Change Is Power! How to Unlock Your Energy Vector

by
John Ross

EBC Publishers
Las Vegas, Nevada

4255 East Charleston Boulevard
Suite 188
Las Vegas, Nevada 89104-6640
800-379-3420

Change Is Power!
How to Unlock Your Energy Vector

by
John Ross

Printed in the United States of America.
ISBN 1-879868-02-4

I Want to Thank ...

First and foremost, I give thanks to my Father in Heaven for everything he has done for me, and to my sweet Kathleen for giving me and my children so much love and understanding. Thank you, Kathleen, for being my wife and believing in me. I also want to thank ...

My angel, Bill Taaffe, for his belief in me. He has been a friend, father, brother, teacher, and mentor to me.

President Bill Clinton, *Success Magazine*, The Olympic Force Committee, and the *Las Vegas Press* for their awards and nominations.

Sherm Day for opening doors and introducing me to Fred Stock, the warden of Atlanta's U.S. Federal Penitentiary.

NationsBank, Home Depot, Kroger Markets, Infiniti, Turner Broadcasting, American Express, Coca Cola, and McDonalds for the previous printings of this book.

All my clients – corporate and individual – who allowed my words to change their lives.

My sister JoAnn for changing and helping me change. She gave me a great example of family and sisterly love.

Steve Osborne for writing an article about me that changed my life. His gifted writing ability has been an ongoing blessing for me.

All those who have gone before me, who made it possible for me to be me.

My parents for loving me and teaching me family values.

My four wonderful children: Lia, Kevin (Budman), Jeffrey (Jeffers), and Janelle (Bellsey). I dreamt about having them from the time I was eight years old, and they have made my dream come true.

All the inmates across the country and the individuals in companies everywhere for believing me, accepting me, listening to my message, and changing their lives.

What People Are Saying
About John Ross and the *Change!* Program

"I am most impressed with your program and with your willingness to share your experiences with those who can most benefit from them.... It appears you have taken the most appropriate step in designing a program aimed at turning lives around: to focus on practical and realizable goals." – S.N., United States Senator

"For the first time in a long time I feel I am in control of my destiny.... I want to thank John Ross for being a true mentor to me in my life." – B.S., gemologist

"It is difficult for me to put into words how much your time has meant to me both financially and on a personal level." – S.G., businessperson

"You and your family of mentors are incredible. You open up your arms and share all of your love, care, and support. Your program *'Change!'* is dynamite because it helps one discover and unleash the wealth of resources that are hidden in all of us." – G.F., businessperson

"John Ross gives you something to take home and apply to almost every aspect of life." – J.R.W., political organization leader

"Many of the guys in here have never believed in themselves. You are just what we need. " – F.P., inmate

"I can't say 'thank you' enough for showing me the way to a better future, not only for myself, but for my entire family." – D.N., businessperson

"It's wonderful to feel so alive. Your are an incredible influence on me. Thank you!" – G.F., businessperson

"A blaze has to start with a spark, and I want to thank you for igniting a spark in me.... You have given me an avenue for my dreams to come true." – P.H., businessperson

"Your proven business savvy, enthusiasm, and motivation touches all." – C.C., president, national business organization

"Anyone can practice the information you teach and grow from it personally and financially. The time I spent with you was probably the most valuable time I've spent as long as I can remember." – G.G., businessperson

"When I went to prison, I thought that I never could be efficient in society and make something of myself. John Ross turned me around 360 degrees. I now have hope that when I return to society, I will make a competent, realistic asset to society." – D.M.B., inmate

"John's presence is so unforgettable.... John is the uncommon man for common folks." – K.B., corporate president

"John's inspiration has been a marvelous blessing in my life." – T.M., real estate investor

"John has given me many different visions, which challenge me to take steps to explore a higher goal in life." – J.H., businessperson

"What a great experience to work one-on-one with John. It is so much easier to grow when you're not fighting your fears.... Thank you John. What a positive experience!" – J.S., businessperson

"Thanks for all your help, advice, and encouragement. I now believe I will succeed." – J.C., businessperson

"Your experience and knowledge will help guide many of us as we make decisions that will affect the rest of our lives." – M.C., president, youth business organization

Introduction

This is a book about change.

Right now, by opening this book, we are changing. Keep reading. Together, we'll explore new possibilities for personal growth, professional success, and lasting, ongoing happiness. It all starts inside – not outside. All we have to do is *Change!* what is waiting there on the inside ... waiting to get out. We need to focus on ourselves internally – not on the external world.

But don't have false expectations. You won't find magic elixirs or secret formulas in this book. What you *will* find is infinitely more powerful: simple ideas and truths that will give us a fresh, new vision of ourselves and our potential. These ideas and truths are not new. (Very few are anymore.) You have probably heard or read them before. But we all need to be reminded of them on a regular basis. And because they are presented here in ways and from perspectives that are perhaps new to you, they will become more understandable, more real, and practical.

Our full potential will reveal itself little by little as we move closer and closer to being our best. Chances are, most people haven't even begun to realize, at this point, how magnificent their true potential really is.

By the way, you will get more out of this book if you first read my autobiography, *Rags to Riches to Rags to Riches*. (If you don't have a copy of it, you can obtain one at no cost by contacting our offices at 1-800-379-3420.) We haven't had the opportunity to grow up together, or go to school together. We don't live across the street from each other, and time is such that we can't sit for hours and get to know each other in person. The

Rags to Riches book was originally a journal that I kept. Later, a gifted writer named Steve Osborne, who has since become my friend, helped me create the book from my journal by excerpting vignettes from it. If you take the time to know where I have come from, and how I learned and continue to learn from my mentors, these pages will have more meaning for you.

I'd like you to do something right now. Write down the answers to the following questions: "Who am I?" "Where do I want to be in my life?" "Where am I right now?" I've provided several lines on the following page to do this. Be sure you take the time to carefully answer these questions. They are crucially important. Remember: "You can't get there from here if the 'here' is not known."

_____

_____

_____

_____

_____

_____

_____

_____

_____

These aren't easy questions. If you don't know how to answer them, you're not alone. Some of my perspectives change every day. But take a few minutes and try to write down some answers anyway. Then, after you've read this book and put into practice even a few of its principles, answer the questions again. I think you'll be amazed by the difference.

The "difference" I'm referring to will come naturally if you open your mind and your heart to the concepts, ideas, and stories you will read in *Change!* These will change many of your perspectives, which will change your attitude about certain things, which in turn will result in changed behavior. I speak inside federal penitentiaries and juvenile detention centers around the country. I've found that most prisoners are there because of their perspectives. (Less than 10 percent of prison inmates are there because of violent crimes.) They think short-term instead of long-term. They focus on today and don't consider tomorrow. This kind of perspective keeps them in jail. But I've found that the moment they change their perspectives and attitudes, their behavior begins to change, and they break out of their mental prisons.

This new behavior is the key to better living, including more rewarding personal and business relationships, increased productivity, and enhanced income.

As I incorporate the teachings and perspectives of my mentors in my own life, I personally see this principle illustrated. I've also seen this principle enhance the lives of hundreds of people I have had the privilege to work with one-on-one, and the thousands who have read this book, heard me speak, or attended one of my training events.

You see, positive change takes place from the inside out. Most companies and individuals that hire me to teach them have a financial focus. Before they can progress, I have to help them understand that they must focus on internal things before anything will significantly change externally, including their incomes. They must change *themselves*. As I mention later in this book, I teach people that one of the easiest ways to start this process of change is to make a dramatic change in their appearance – the way they dress, the length of their hair, and so on. This opens the door to deeper, more internal changes from within.

I think I know why you're reading this book. You know you can be more than you are today – that you can do more, do better, and achieve greater things. You believe there can be more to life.

You've probably been feeling like you're in a rut, or that you've reached a plateau. Maybe you're trying to change yourself and your patterns. But you're not sure you know how. Or you can't maintain the enthusiasm and motivation to do so. Perhaps you think that life isn't fair, or that almost everyone else is happier and better off than you.

If any of these feelings are yours, I want you to know that you are not unlike most people, myself included. You *are* different, however, in one very important way: you have made the choice, like me, by opening this book, to do something to change your situation.

Choice and *change*. Those two words imply risk. And they demand the courage to face that risk.

I wrote this book for you and for me, and for people like us who want more out of life and are willing to take the risk to get it. The principles and strategies contained in these pages can help us thoroughly enjoy our lives and be happy, wealthy, healthy, and fulfilled by working to be our own *Personal Best*.

"Personal Best" is a wonderful phrase. It is our own special key to a world of prosperity, opportunity, and happiness.

But how do we become our *Personal Best*, and where do we start? First, we must understand that it's a process – a journey. Our best is not a place, nor a destination. It's a lifelong, continuous process – just like breathing.

The illusion that success is a place or final destination has been the cause of many great failures. People work hard to get to this "destination," and at some point they feel as if they've "arrived," and they stop reaching. But the minute they stop reaching, they begin losing. This is true with many facets of life – money, marriage, business, weight loss, fitness, and so on. This illusive "destination" evaporates like a mirage in the desert before we can ever reach it. We shouldn't keep reaching for that mirage – that place which doesn't exist. Instead, we should start reaching inside ourselves to find our own paths to our Personal Best.

I wrote this book to help us on our Personal Best journey, and to lead us down new and exciting paths of excellence.

My challenge is to embrace the ideas in this book with an open heart and mind. As we put them to work, we'll soon find that we're truly achieving more and actually enjoying life more than we ever have before. Our lives will begin to change, transform, and evolve. That's a promise.

One important point: if you run into something in this book that you can't accept or don't fully understand, don't worry. Leave it and go on ... for now. I don't want you to blindly accept anything I've written in this book if it doesn't feel right for you at this point in your life. I also don't want you to disregard the major ideas in this book because of a difference in a few details.

Don't throw any idea away. Instead, put it on a shelf in your mind marked "Ideas I'm Not Sure About." Then move on. Don't pass final judgement on the idea one way or the other. At some point in the future, that "shelved" idea might suddenly make sense or become "right" and help you leap a hurdle or progress further. If that happens, the idea will be waiting there for you on the shelf.

Please don't underestimate the importance of reading this or any other "self-improvement" book. Too many people think, "It's just a book." But a book is a collection of organized thoughts, and thoughts rule our minds, and our minds reign over every other part of our beings.

Everything we do – every action we take – begins with a thought. It's amazing but true. Imagine what we can accomplish when we begin to harness and control the power of our thoughts!

What percentage of our brains do you suppose we use? Experts say we only use 5 to 10 percent of their capacity. I believe, however, that we can tap into the other 90 to 95 percent by changing our perspectives and exercising our thinking. We tend to stop expanding our mental capacity when we leave school – to stop reading and learning because we get so bogged down with life. There is, after all, only so much time available to us, and unfortunately we don't have much time for ourselves after meeting the demands of our families, careers, and other responsibilities. But if we can take just a little time every so often and focus on learning to change our perspectives, we'll maximize our time and our potential, and we *will* grow and progress.

That's what this book is all about. If you are sincere in your desire to change as you read it, these simple thoughts will blossom into action, and grow into mighty oaks of self-fulfillment. Whether we're employees or business owners, teachers or students, doctors or cab drivers, we can't grow unless we change. It's like Zig Ziglar says: "If you keep doing what you've been doing, you will keep getting what you've been getting." Let's work to change what we're doing so we can change what we're getting in all aspects of our lives.

That's the secret of *Change!* It opens the gateway to our own greatest potential. It helps us become our Personal Best ... from the inside out.

Before You Start Reading ...

To open a locked door, we need a key. To unlock our full potential and change, we need a series of keys. This book contains 11 keys, each of which in turn contains a series of segments, or "nuggets" of thought, like notches on a key. Some are short and to the point. Others take a more explaining. Each nugget is a complete thought that we need to take time to digest.

As these segments are read, be sure to take notes and underline or highlight sentences or sections that have particular importance. Write thoughts in the margins. Jot down plans and changes for commitment on a blank sheet at the back of the book.

As you read, you'll occasionally be asked to spend a few minutes away from the book to write down your thoughts. Please do this. Don't rush. Focus! By jotting down our thoughts, we can measure our achievements and assess the changes we will be making. If we don't write our thoughts down, we may not be fully aware of the progress we will make.

Before we start, I'd like to share a few thoughts....

"I am only one, but still I am one. I cannot do everything, but still I can do something. And because I cannot do everything I will not refuse to do the something that I can do."
— Edward Everett Hale

"I believe in miracles because I am one."
— John Lucas, former NBA player and San Antonio Spurs coach.

"Few burdens are heavy when everybody lifts."
— African Proverb

The Man in the Glass
When you get what you want in your struggle for self
and the world makes you king for a day,
Just go to the mirror and look at yourself
and see what the man has to say.
For it isn't your parents, your children, or wife
who judgement upon you must pass,
The fellow whose verdict counts most in your life
is the one staring back from the glass.
Some people may think you're a straight-shooting chum
and call you a wonderful guy,
But the man in the glass says you're only a bum
if you can't look him straight in the eye.
He's the fellow to please, never mind all the rest,
for he's with you clear up to the end.
And you've passed your most dangerous, difficult test
if the man in the glass is your friend.
You may fool the whole world down the pathway of life
and get pats on your back as you pass,
But your final reward will be heartaches and tears,
if you've cheated the man in the glass.
— Anonymous (Phil Bonadonna, a friend, gave this to me.)

"Change reality, but never lie to yourself."
— John Ross

Table of Contents

Key 1:

GETTING READY FOR CHANGE

Dig Deep, Then Reach for the Sky

If you were to walk up to me today and say, "John, I want to build a skyscraper of success that will rise high into the clouds, and I want you to tell me where to begin," I would give you a shovel and say, "Dig a deep hole."

Granted, when you're excited to climb quickly toward success, digging a hole in the opposite direction is the last thing you want to do. But it must be done. You can't rise to great heights – and stay there – without first digging deep.

You see, there *is* such a thing as "instant success," and there *is* such a thing as "lasting success," but there is *no* such thing as "instant, lasting success." True success that endures is a slow and ongoing process. You can't make it happen overnight.

It's like building a skyscraper. Imagine what would happen if the contractor was in a hurry to build a high-rise and decided to take a shortcut and skip the foundation. Long before the building would have reached its height potential, it would have begun leaning, if it hadn't already tumbled down. There is no way such a building could ever stand the test of time. A strong wind or storm would quickly topple it, or the instability of its mass on the unreinforced ground would eventually cause its demise.

When I consult with individuals, and especially newly formed companies, they invariably want to start making money immediately. The old axiom is appropriate here: "You can give a man a fish and feed him for a day. But if you teach a man to fish, you've fed him for a lifetime."

The first strategy is the quick-fix approach. The second strategy – teaching the man how to fish – requires the time and effort necessary to build a foundation of knowledge and skill. It won't happen overnight, but the rewards will last a lifetime.

I remind my clients that the object of the training I give them is a lifetime of success. I'm not training them to merely succeed or just get by. I'm not training them to make some quick bucks. Too many people think they can beat the system and sneak around the principles of success and get what they want *now*. Invariably, they end up "paying dues."

I know. I wanted to rush through everything. I wanted to be the first kid on the block to become rich and famous. Then one day I realized that I hadn't taken the time to create a strong foundation. And I certainly was moving too fast to "stop and smell the daisies," as my dad used to say. Life soon taught me the lesson that it is vital to formulate a strong and deep foundation first.

More and more people are learning – like I did – that quick fixes don't work. (Or if they work for awhile, they don't last). Sure, digging a hole for a proper foundation seems counter-productive to constructing a building. However, without that foundation, the slightest challenge will topple the greatest structure.

So it is with business and life in general. We are challenged day in and day out. We are placed in the pressure cooker of stress. We are presented with choices that have to be made, often spontaneously. When we're challenged, stressed, or forced to make difficult and immediate decisions, we'd better have a firm foundation, or our skyscraper of success will come tumbling down around us. What we are inside becomes very visible in these situations. Without a solid foundation, we cannot endure the test of time.

Can you imagine a farmer trying to rush the growing process? Impossible. He must do it the right way and at the right time. Then, and only then, will he reap the rewards of his work. It's a fundamental law of nature. I'm sure we all understand this on a gut level, but we tend to forget it. Why? One reason is because of today's society, and its continuous repetition of clever advertising, which perpetuates the myth that we can obtain things quickly and easily.

If you know my story, or if you've read about me in the book, *Rags to Riches to Rags to Riches*, you're familiar with some of what I've experienced. I had everything I could have wanted and then lost it all, except my health and my belief in myself. And I came awfully close to losing those, too.

If anyone wanted to get back on top quickly, I did.

I could have told myself a hundred times a day that I deserved to have success *now*. But, would that have altered the natural and fundamental principle that good things take time? No!

No matter how badly I wanted to be successful again, the forces of nature wouldn't compress the amount of time, effort, and dedication I had to invest to regain wealth and success. By seeking shortcuts, by trying to rise without first digging a deep foundation, all I would have found is frustration and disappointment. I would have become disillusioned. I would have driven away the very success I was so desperately seeking.

Good things do take time.

A nationally recognized author, teacher, and motivator, Stephen R. Covey, uses a wonderful analogy. He points out that we can't forget to plant in the spring, and still expect to harvest in the fall. We can hope all we want, but it won't make the crops come up when we want them to. The only way to get what we want is to follow a specific, effective plan that we've established for our success.

We must decide what we really want, develop a plan, and *stick to it* until our desires become realities. What I'm talking about here is the power of long-term thinking. It's one of the great keys to unlocking our potential and changing our lives.

In the first section of this book, or "key," I offer you my thoughts, feelings, and philosophies regarding what it takes to become personally ready inside. This section deals with personal development – what to think, things to do, and perspective changes that will open our minds and direct our thinking into a more creative and motivated framework.

The aspects we discuss here, in my opinion, are some of the most important elements – the foundation – of success. When consulting with individuals, I make these principles the immediate focus. This sets the stage for everything else we discuss.

We should spend as much time as possible as we begin our quest for success focusing on the principles in this section. In the same way that a contractor starts his building with a strong foundation, these truths will give us the firm footing we need to build our high-rise of success.

Remember:
•   A firm, solid foundation is vital in all we do.
•   Good things do take time. Enjoy the process.

Marathon Vision

In Salt Lake City there's a marathon every spring that winds its way from the city streets up into the mountain canyons, and then back down into the city. It's grueling.

For the last several years a man who is now in his 40s has run the race, and has become somewhat of a celebrity – not because he wins, but because he comes in dead last year after year. In fact, he not only finishes last, he staggers in long after the bandstands at the finish line have been disassembled and the litter from the post-race festivities has been cleaned up.

One television news team interviewed him a few years ago while he was lumbering alone down the canyon as the day grew old. The reporter asked the overweight and exhausted marathon runner what his secret to failure was. He gave all the credit to a lack of training. (Actually, that was not completely true. A friend of mine knows this individual. He told me that in reality, he *does* train: two days before the race he walks around his block twice. Then, on the day before the race, he eats a package of Twinkies.)

Obviously, the more sensible approach for this marathon runner would be to take the time to seriously train for the race. He might have begun by running one mile, or even just a half mile each day, depending on his personal level of fitness (which was almost non-existent). Then, over time, he could have slowly built up his endurance and speed. Plus, he could have eaten right. Soon, he would have been able to run three miles. Then five. Eventually, he would have developed the physical stamina to run a full marathon and cross the finish line before the crowd went home.

Equally important, he would have instilled in his mind the belief that he *could* run a marathon within a decent time because he would have invested the time necessary to prepare. He would have known what his body could have done ... and how he would have felt at certain points along the way.

This principle applies to us in whatever endeavors we undertake. That's because our minds, along with our bodies, are built on the foundation of the successes (and sometimes failures) of each previous day and experience.

To strengthen our bodies, we must exercise and build them up. That's simply a law of nature. And there's an equally irrefutable law that governs how we strengthen and develop our minds. We build our mind in basically the same way we build our muscles: by exercising them. Most people stop exercising their mental capacity regularly after they graduate from school.

Reading is a wonderful mind exerciser. I failed in that regard for several years after my school years were over. Then my mentor taught me the value of reading. Since then, I've developed a love for the written word.

Another way to exercise the mind is to engage in valuable conversations with our mentors, or people who have different perspectives than we do. Too often, I thought my perspective was the right one, only to learn the hard way that I did not have all the answers. We can learn from the experiences of others – especially our mentors. The value of a mentor is lifelong. We can grow and progress by leaps and bounds by simply conversing with our mentors.

Yet another way to exercise our minds is to listen to tapes. When we're in our cars driving to and from work or the store, or on trips, tapes offer a passive, easy way to gain concepts, information, and new perspectives. This "exercise" technique is too often overlooked, and the radio is turned on instead. I'm not suggesting that we should listen to tapes every moment we're in the car, but if we remember to utilize this technique, it's amazing how much we can learn, and how fast we can learn it.

There are other ways to exercise our "mental muscles," of course. Once we accept the concept that our minds must be worked in order to grow, we'll devise other creative ways to give them the exercise they need, no matter how busy we are.

Most of us have no idea what our minds can do. Still, we expect success to be simple and immediate. But, like the running of a marathon, true success and genuine change cannot be achieved overnight.

Yet it *can* be achieved.

Remember:
- Exercise your body and your mind.
- Start small and slow, then build up.

Every Little Step We Take

In the movie, *"What About Bob?"* Bill Murray plays a character who is struggling to find his identity. Under the not-so-willing guidance of his psychiatrist (played by Richard Dreyfuss), the patient learns to overcome his fears by taking "baby steps."

If we look beyond the comedy, we'll find a surprisingly simple message that is actually very powerful: We don't change our lives by taking dramatic, drastic leaps. Change comes through a series of small, constant improvements.

These are "baby steps."

The Japanese also teach and practice this principle. They call it *kaizen*, which means "constant, tiny improvements." It underlies much of Japan's progress and success over the years. *Kaizen* teaches that all people should constantly make tiny improvements in every aspect of their lives. This does not mean physical things alone. It means absolutely everything.

In other words, if I haven't seen you for a year, I should be able to look at you and immediately notice significant changes. These changes would not necessarily relate only to your outward appearance, though they could. More importantly, they would be internal changes that have become manifested in your external appearance – in your face, your walk, your voice, in the confident expression in your eyes.

These changes would mean that you are constantly in the process of becoming a new and better person. You are changing and growing. You are improving yourself in a variety of ways. You don't accept complacency. You are adjusting yourself all the time.

In relationships, sometimes things don't work out, and we don't know why. On the other hand, sometimes relationships are successful, and again, we can't put our fingers on the specific reason for it. I believe that this has a lot to do with a special, personal magnetism that we can build up within ourselves over time if we focus on it. The better we feel about ourselves, the more powerful this magnetism becomes. As it becomes more powerful, our relationships become more successful and things seem to work out better where other people are involved. One of the most important keys to creating this personal magnetism is *kaizen* – making tiny, constant improvements in ourselves that build us up and enhance us on an ongoing basis.

Kaizen is vital to the Japanese way of thinking, and it is obviously carried throughout their business thinking as well.

Whatever you call it, the idea works.

To accomplish the goals that are important to us, we must begin by exercising our minds and our vision. That's one of the major goals of this book: to help us reshape our vision through the achievement of small, measurable steps along the way. After all, even a marathon begins with one step.

It's exciting to know that although it takes time to build our skyscraper of success, we will be able to see and feel the positive results of the steps we are taking almost immediately. Each day, we should put one or two ideas to work, and we'll begin to see some amazing results from our efforts sooner than we might expect.

Remember:
- Take baby steps.
- Make consistent, tiny improvements.

Marathon Mindset

It takes time to build our vision. It's best to start slowly.

We should begin with a goal that is small and easily attainable. Once we've succeeded, we'll be able to set our sights on progressively larger and more challenging goals.

Our "marathon mindset" will even make big goals easier to achieve. We should break down our goals into small steps, treat each step like a goal, reach the first step, and enjoy our success. We then move on to the next step, and the next, until we have reached our ultimate goals.

A common mistake is to focus only on the "big idea." We may have great visions and try to achieve them all at once. Unfortunately, tackling a "big idea" is like eating an elephant. When we realize how much is ahead of us, we become discouraged and quit.

It *is* possible to eat an elephant ... *if* we take it one bite at a time. Similarly, it's possible to achieve our greatest visions *if* we take them one step at a time. But it's essential to enjoy each bite, or each step, along the way. The rewards we give ourselves after each step will fuel our continued progress. Sure, we need the vision of our long-term goals to keep ourselves directed, but we should never get so wrapped up in the long-term prize that we don't fully enjoy the rewards of our short-term goals – the stepping stones that keep us motivated and moving.

The goal of losing weight is a good example. Professional weight-loss counselors know that it is virtually impossible for clients to successfully lose weight if they focus only on the "big goal." So they break it down into weekly goals and chart a path for success.

Just imagine what might happen if we had a goal to lose 50 pounds. Our first week, we might struggle and lose two or three pounds. Instead of being elated, we'd still see ourselves far from our goal. We'd be overwhelmed, physically and mentally. Chances are high that we would not succeed.

But by breaking down our big goal into weekly steps, we'd no longer be visualizing a 50-pound goal. Instead, we might have a goal to lose two pounds during the first week. So, rather than being discouraged with a weight loss of two or three pounds, we'd be pleased. And we'd be motivated to stay on track.

Why does this work? Trying to see (and achieve) a long-term goal, fully, right from the start is counterproductive because it is unbelievable – not necessarily on a logical level, but on a deeper experiential level. The goal is such a long way from where we are right now that in our minds it becomes unattainable.

By breaking a big goal down into small chunks, we don't have to push beyond our ability to believe in ourselves. If we can actually visualize achieving each successive goal, we can then fully believe in our ability to reach them.

At each level our vision will change, advance, and evolve. So will our perspective. It's much like coming into the light from a darkened room – our eyes will open wider and wider to our true potential.

We are beginning to *Change!*

Remember:
- Break all goals into tiny, achievable steps.
- Start today!

Don't Worry About Home Runs

For now, I want you to throw out any thoughts of becoming a millionaire. By the way, I'm talking about being a millionaire in terms of real income – not on paper. We all know that there are a lot of "paper millionaires" around who couldn't rub two $10 bills together.

If your annual *net* (take-home) income doesn't currently exceed $100,000, don't try to imagine earning $1 million right now. Start with $100,000 and work up.

One key to success is to deal with reality. If you are 45 years old and have not made more than $50,000 a year, moving up to $100,000 is a real jump – double the highest amount you have ever earned in your life. Making $1 million is miles away.

Remember when you played baseball for the first time? If you were well coached, you didn't get up to the plate and try to hit a home run. You simply wanted to meet the ball and get on base. That's the way to win games and have a good batting average.

Too many people grow up and expect to hit home runs in their personal lives whenever they step up to the plate – even when they haven't worked out and practiced regularly. They swing like wild men and then get discouraged and yell and get angry when they don't hit "grand slams" in their financial lives.

Don't make that mistake. You need to start small and work your way up. Get hits and get on base. Understand that going from $25,000 a year to $50,000, or from $50,000 to $100,000 requires a 100 percent change. That's major. Are you ready for it?

A client of mine who lifts weights went into a gym and bench-pressed 200 pounds. That was the most he had ever bench-pressed in his life. His current annual take-home income was $35,000. That was the most he had ever earned in his life. He may have thought that setting a financial goal of earning $70,000 a year was not enough. So I drew his attention to the fact that increasing his income to $70,000 would be like increasing his bench press to 400 pounds. (Using the algebraic equation, "A:B::C:D," we find that "200lbs : 400lbs :: $35,000 : $70,000." In short, the ratio between the two pairs of numbers is the same.)

That put the task in perspective for him. When we put income in that perspective, the difficulty of doubling it becomes clearer. In fact, it can be overwhelming to the point that it seems impossible, and therefore deadens the motivation to make it happen. That's why I find it so interesting that so many people think it should be easy to dramatically increase their incomes, when at the same time they would consider it impossible to run twice as far as the longest race they ever ran, cut their golf handicap in half, or increase their performance 100 percent in any other measurable sport.

Our society's attitude of unrealistic expectations, to me, has been caused to a great extent by the "get-rich-quick" gurus on television. (It seems that the only people getting rich are the gurus who are selling the books and tapes.) They say it's easy. They say that if *they* could do it *anyone* can. That's one of the biggest lies in the world! Making money is not easy. There are ways to make it simple, but it never was and never will be easy.

So let's not set ourselves up for discouragement and failure right out of the chute. If we want to double our best financial success so far, let's set smaller, more realistic goals that will serve as stepping stones along the way. With work and effort, we can double our current income by taking it one step at a time.

When we do, *then* it will be time to pursue our financial home runs!

Remember:
- Don't worry about hitting home runs at this point. Just get on base.

- Be realistic. A 100 percent improvement requires a 100 percent change.

Gravity Release

Almost everything we do demands the greatest effort at the very start. Even the simple act of getting up out of a chair requires a burst of energy to move us off the cushion. Once we're moving, the rest is relatively easy.

Rockets expend 90 percent of their thrust, power, and fuel just to break through the relatively thin layer of atmosphere that envelopes our world. Once beyond it, the remaining 10 percent of their energy is enough to propel them millions of miles into space, and then bring them home again.

This principle of gravity release applies to our everyday lives as much as it does to the physical world of rocket science. It is as much a mental and emotional law as it is a physical law.

To overcome our own "gravity," we must understand that effort and changes must be made. Dramatic alterations must occur, and the most difficult part of this journey of self-improvement is the first part.

We need to prepare our minds for this, expect it, and embrace it. It will take the majority of our strength and energy in the beginning stages to get ourselves going. We should expect difficulty and struggles.

If you're currently earning in the neighborhood of $50,000 a year, think of your personal "atmosphere" as being the $100,000 annual income figure. Expect to use 90 percent of your energy just getting yourself to that level. Once there, you'll be in a position to utilize your momentum to perpetuate your income and enjoy true financial growth and stability.

Whatever you do, don't give up. Realize that the pull of gravity will be strongest in the early stages of any endeavor. With every step we take, with every level we rise, it will become easier, and we will become freer from the forces pulling us back.

Eventually we will break through to a place where gravity cannot bind us.

The key is to persevere. Stick with it. What a waste it would be if a rocket were to use 89 percent of its fuel and then turn back just a few miles short of breaking through the atmosphere! Yet people do this all the time. Salesmen give up just one call short of that million-dollar sale. Writers give up just one novel short of a best-seller. Inventors give up just one attempt shy of creating the innovation of the decade.

When I had to start over again in life, I was fortunate to meet several business people that had done the same thing I was trying to do: overcome adversity and attain success. These people had persevered long enough to blast through the dense gravity of their personal atmospheres. They told me their stories. After hearing what they had had to go through, I didn't feel so horrible about my own situation, which wasn't nearly as bad as theirs had been.

I remember one of them had been forced to live in his pick-up truck for several months *with his wife and children.* When I imagined that grim situation, and realized that they overcame it, I knew I could endure what I had been going through.

The key is to know that others have gone before us and have overcome the same if not greater difficulties and setbacks. Knowing that, we can persist and keep pushing to make it back again (or to make it the first time).

The concept of persevering until we achieve "gravity release" brings to mind examples of several famous people who overcame barriers and stumbling blocks because they didn't give up.

Arrested Development, a musical group, named their first album "3 Years 5 Months & 2 Days in the Life of ... " because that's how long it took them to get their first album released. They immediately won two Grammies (the first rap group to win in the new artist category) as well as MTV, NAACP Image, and Soul Train awards. They took top honors in the *Village Voice*'s

Jazz & Pop and *Rolling Stone*'s critic's polls. A year after its release, their first album had sold 2.5 million copies. It was in the top ten album list, with three hits in the top ten.

What if they had given up? What if they had thrown in the towel after three years, five months, and *one* day? Was persistence worth it? You tell me.

Walt Disney went bankrupt seven times before making it big. Madonna was crying in a hotel stairwell just months before skyrocketing to success, thinking she would never make it. Abraham Lincoln suffered numerous defeats before being elected President of the United States of America. The movie, *Star Wars*, was turned down by every major motion picture company in the United States, all of which said it would never do well. Its phenomenal success is now a matter of motion picture history.

I could relate example after example of similar stories. What is the common thread that runs through each of them? The answer is simple: persistence. It is persistence that breaks through the atmospheric barrier that holds so many people back. It is persistence that empowers some people to reach their goals while so many others fall short ... often just one mile, one day, or one last attempt short of breaking through.

With perseverance and patience, success *will* come. Any sales manager in the telemarketing or door-to-door sales industry will tell you that. They know that sales are generally a function of numbers – that a sales person will get several "no's" before getting a "yes." They know that it is just a matter of time before someone says "yes" to the sales offer. And they will tell you that the reason why one person makes it in sales and another fails is perseverance. Most people give up because they get discouraged when success doesn't come quickly. If they don't see immediate rewards, they quit and try something else.

Truly successful people are generally those who say, "I will persevere *until* I get what I want, no matter how long it takes."   When I started over again, I made a commitment to myself that I would never, under any circumstances, ever give up. I was going to make it again no matter how long it took or what I had to do. I was going to hang in there. After making that commitment, I didn't have to think about it any more. My success was then simply a function of time.

I am often asked how to develop or achieve the attitude I just described. One way is to read and learn about successful people that have overcome failure in their lives on the way to the success they now enjoy. When you read about these people, you will realize that they are normal people just like you and me, and you will think, "Hey, if they can do it, so can I!"

Colonel Sanders was one of those inspirational people. He went out time and time again to sell his chicken recipe after he turned 65 years old only to be turned down repeatedly. He surely felt discouraged. But he refused to accept his defeats as final and eventually became one of the wealthiest men in America, thanks to that often rejected recipe ... and his refusal to give up.

One last note about perseverance: we've got to believe that what we're trying to do is possible, and that we can actually accomplish it. Roger Banister believed that the human body was capable of propelling itself a mile in less than four minutes. Yet no one in history had ever done it. In fact, the prevailing opinion – even among the scientific and medical communities at that time – held that the human body was not physically capable of running a mile in less than four minutes.

Banister believed that it *was* possible, and that he could do it. He refused to listen to those who told him he was attempting the impossible. The result? He became the first human in history to break the four-minute mile barrier.

Interestingly, once he proved that it was possible, several other runners broke through the four-minute mile barrier within a year's time! And now, if you don't run a mile in less than four minutes, you're not even in the race.

What happened? The runners hadn't changed physically. They weren't in better shape. They hadn't learned any new techniques to make them run faster. The difference was in their beliefs. They suddenly knew that it *could* be done, so they went out and did it. Before Banister, their disbelief had formed an insurmountable barrier between them and their goal.

So let's have faith that we can accomplish our goal, then make a commitment to persevere until we do. If we do, it will happen!

Remember:
- The hardest part is getting started.
- Don't give up. It gets easier.
- Perseverance is critical to success.

Don't Conform to the Norm

Herbert Hoover once said, "I never met a father and mother who did not want their children to grow up to be uncommon men and women ... for the future of America rests not in mediocrity."

Hoover was right. Mediocrity is not what the future of America needs. And it's not what *our* futures need, either.

Do we want to be "average"? Do we want to be just like the other 99 percent of the people in the world who don't even come close to exercising all their potential? Do we want to base our thoughts and actions on the "norm"? Do we want to follow the ways of the average and commonplace, and walk the path of the mediocre person who doesn't make an effort to rise above where or what he or she currently is?

If we want more for ourselves, then we're going to have to break out of the norm. If we don't want to be average, we're going to have to be *different*.

By *different*, I don't mean "odd" or "strange" just for the sake of standing out. What I'm referring to is the quality of being completely ourselves, and developing our own unique capabilities, personalities, and talents, even though those may be very different than what society has stamped "normal and ordinary."

In short, I want you to be *you* and me to be *me*. That's the only way we're ever going to become all that we are capable of being.

Although society, by its nature, wants its members to "fit the mold," it paradoxically reserves its greatest rewards for those who shun mediocrity and break that mold. The people who make the most money, hold the highest positions, influence the most lives, and live the most preferred lifestyles in our society are those who dare to be different. Look at people like Steven Speilberg and Ross Perot – people who have excelled in their fields and made real contributions. For people like these, "the norm" was never good enough.

Our first challenge is to see ourselves as people who are, in fact, different. We must first accept the idea that we are not just average people. Then we must take the initiative to rise to our highest levels of excellence.

We must banish the "most people" myth from our minds. When I told my sister that I was going to write a book and travel around the country speaking about it, she told me that "most people" don't make money on the books they write. My response was that I am not "most people." Then I began to think of all the things I've done that "most people" haven't done. Most people have never made over $1,000,000 a year. Most people have never created their own successful business with over 20 employees. Most people have not come back from zero. Most people have not been millionaires. Most people have not been featured on the evening news' feature story for one week straight. Most people have not spent years listening to positive tapes and reading the best books. And the list went on.

We can all come up with lists of things we've done and do that set us apart from "most people" and make us unique. Therefore, we should never let ourselves be sidetracked or stopped by the fact that "most people" can't or wouldn't do what we want to accomplish. We simply aren't "most people."

Once we see ourselves as *extra*ordinary individuals, our new way of thinking will become dramatically different from most others around us. We'll see our lives in a new light. Our attitudes, our perspectives, and our level of prosperity will evolve. We will begin to realize how negative most people are, and hopefully we'll work to surround ourselves with positive people who are also working to improve themselves.

Becoming a unique individual is not necessarily easy. Many people today consider anything that is different to be strange, weird, or abnormal. I prefer the terms "unique," "original," "uncommon," "singular," or "distinctive." Those terms make being different sound more socially acceptable.

But on the other hand, we shouldn't be afraid of being a bit crazy at times. In Tom Peters' books, *Liberation Management* and *The Pursuit of Wow!*, he talks about the importance of being zany or crazy. He says that the only way companies are going to make it today is if they hire leaders that are "bonkers" and are willing to do things outside the norm.

Take Herb Kelleher of Southwest Airlines as an example. He was once dismissed as an oddity. However, Southwest Airlines is now soaring while the others are struggling. His airline often won't give passengers assigned seats, refuses to transfer baggage, crams passengers into seats, and serves crackers and cookies for lunch. Its tickets are not sold through the industry's computerized reservation system. And it avoids flying to many large airports.

How does Southwest Airlines make it? By keeping costs at rock-bottom. By flying high-frequency, one-hour flights loaded with people. By not offering amenities that add up to millions of dollars that customers could care less about. The airline broke out of the mold, refused to listen to analysts that said it would not make it, and has made a nice niche for itself. Herb Kelleher and his airline have not conformed to the norm.

When IBM was looking for a new chief executive, the search committee's main criteria for the position was vision – not necessarily any experience in the computer industry. More important for the members of the committee were vision, charisma, and a savvy sense of business. These people wanted someone who could break out of the mold and be truly creative.

A wise man once said, "Some observers have been led to comment on a 'childlike' or 'primitive' quality in a creative individual. He is childlike and primitive in the sense that he has not been trapped by the learned rigidities that immobilize the rest of us."

Being unique pays off. It's as simple as that. Consider the dandelion. Actually, it's beautiful. But we think of it as a weed that should be killed, rather than a flower that should be grown and cultivated.

Why? Because it's so common.

Don't be common. Don't force yourself to conform to society's mold. Be unique. Let your own talents and capabilities blossom. Dare to be different!

Remember:
- Weird is good.
- See yourself as the unique person you are.

Never Settle for Less

Once we've taken the giant step of daring to be different, and rejecting the idea that we're just "average" people, we must make a commitment to settle for nothing less than what we really want to achieve and be.

Too often we settle for too little. We complacently accept where we are, what we are, and what life has dealt us. Rather than fighting, we accept life as it is – rather than the way it *could be*.

It's amazing how the world can teach us to drift so far into the woodwork of life that we become virtually unnoticed. It's too easy to melt into obscurity in school, in big corporations, and in life in general.

We even begin to believe that if we don't make waves, everything will be fine and we'll just drift through our existences. But who wants to just drift?

Don't be afraid to make waves for the right reasons, whether those reasons are large or small. Here's an example of a small reason: you're at a restaurant, and the rare steak you ordered comes back medium well done. Would you send it back? Or would you meekly accept it, not wanting to make waves? Sure, it's no big deal. Or is it? Such attitudes generally express themselves in bigger ways.

Too many people too readily accept lives that are "medium well done" when they really wanted them "rare."

If we want to live rare lives, we can't be afraid to ask for what we want, demand our rights, and yes, even make tidal waves if that becomes necessary. Remember, we don't get what we don't ask for.

The simple act of *asking* contains great power. When we ask for something and someone tells us, "We don't normally do that," do we merely accept that answer? Or do we ask one further question: "I realize you don't normally do this, but could you make an exception here?"

Let's get in the habit of looking beyond what is average and normal and common, and ask for what we want. If we go to a restaurant and the table to which you are taken is not to our liking, we should ask for the one we want. Why accept what we don't want? Every day of our lives, we will find a variety of ways to utilize this simple principle.

The key is to begin to reject accepting that which is just average. Let's demand the best from others ... *and* from ourselves.

Remember:
- Ask for what you want.
- Accept nothing less than the best.

Being True to Ourselves

Inside each of us is the person we truly are – an individual who wants to express himself or herself as a unique human being with individual dispositions, gifts, and desires.

Unfortunately, society, friends, members of our families, and business associates try to influence us in ways that cause us to not be true to ourselves. This is a common human malady. We find ourselves living our lives for others, conforming to beliefs, behaviors, and goals that are not our own. We tend to value the opinions of others over our own. We seek approval from outside sources, rather than from within. All the while, we feel like square pegs in a round-holed world. No wonder. There is no way to attain real happiness under those conditions.

In order to reach our full potentials, we must stop lying to ourselves, face reality, and take Shakespeare's advice: "To thine own self be true." This means being completely ourselves in our mannerisms, dress, activities, habits, and beliefs.

We will never be completely happy or fulfilled if we try to live someone else's life. An imitation can be, at best, second best.

When we let the people we really are come out, we will begin to manifest ourselves in ways that will bring us closer to success. When we stifle our true selves, we create inner turmoil and drive success away from us.

A free mind is a creative mind. A creative mind is a happy, prosperous mind.

Let's live our lives *for* ourselves, *as* ourselves. This is not selfish. In fact, the greatest gift we can offer our family, friends, and clients is our true selves. Betraying our true selves never works – even in business. People will feel that we are uncomfortable with ourselves, and they in turn will not want to do business with us. Deals will fall through for no apparent reason.

I often meet people who are so stiff and artificial that they can't relax. They act as though they're on stage all the time. This is because they're trying to pretend they're someone they aren't. They're putting on false airs. It's as if they are trying so hard to make everybody else happy that they've forgotten about themselves, and lost touch with their own identity and individuality.

Some of the most successful and prosperous people are those who refuse to play the game of life by others' rules. I find it fascinating that Sam Walton, the founder of the Wal-Mart dynasty, drove an old pick-up truck when he could have driven any kind of car he wanted. Bill Marriott, founder of Marriott Corporation and Hotels, has chosen to drive a station wagon for years. Ross Perot drives a simple, basic American car.

These super-successes could easily have fallen into the "system," but they decided to be true to themselves and not let anyone or anything control them. They decided to play the game by their own rules. They had the courage to "walk to the tune of a different drummer" as Henry David Thoreau put it.

When I go to a consulting or speaking job, I sometimes shock people because they expect to see me dressed in a suit and tie. But for me, that would be too restrictive and formal. I went to a Catholic grade school and high school. I had to wear a suit and tie every day. It's difficult for me to wear them now. Instead, I generally wear what's comfortable. I want to have my mind, both on a conscious and subconscious level, free to concentrate on what I am there to do: help my clients. I don't want to be thinking about wrinkling my coat or staining my tie.

But that's me.

You might feel more "you" in a three-piece suit. Great! I admire you. You see, you need to find out who *you* are. Most people don't know. They've lived so long under the wings of their parents, or an overbearing spouse, or an individuality-stifling boss that they've never taken the time to stop and think about their own inner preferences and potentials.

Don't make that mistake. Take the time today (*right now*) to think about who you really are. Then take action. Have the courage to *be* you. Dress according to your own tastes and style. If you're a "suit person," wear a suit. If you're a casual person, dress casual. Don't go against your grain. Granted, you may have to adhere to certain dress codes at work, in school, or when you go to church, but you'd be surprised how you can tailor most dress codes to mold to your individual style.

If you like your hair long, wear it long! Want a mustache just for the sake of having one? Grow one! Always, always, always be true to yourself.

I promise you that by getting in touch with yourself and by finding out who the *real you* is, you'll automatically feel better. And that will naturally bring about more happiness and success in your life and in the lives of those around you.

Remember:
- Be true to yourself.
- Express yourself.

Looking For Short Cuts?

I remember when I took my first typing class in high school. Our instructor told us not to look at the keys when we worked on our tutorials. Of course I knew I could go faster if I looked, so I did. As a result I won many of our school's typing contests and felt very good about my awesome typing abilities.

But in the long run I was short-changing myself. Sure, I was ahead of the rest of the class initially, but after a while they caught up and then surpassed me. Why? They weren't cheating. They were following the instructions of those who had gone before them and knew better.

But not me. I decided *I* knew better, and for a time I was successful. But I could have done much better if I had learned the right way the first time. Today, I can type 65+ words per minute and I no longer have to look at the keys. But it took me years of diligence, patience, and persistence in following the proper teachings to relearn to type the right way. It was much more difficult for me to replace a bad habit with a good one than it would have been to have put in the time and effort to learn it right in the first place. That experience taught me a great lesson: *The easy way is seldom the best way*. In other words, we shouldn't take short cuts! They are not worth taking. A short cut may appear to be an attractive "quick fix," but there's always a price to pay. Sure, we can often find short cuts, but they will rarely get us where we want to go and keep us there long enough to enjoy it. Remember, genuine success is a process, not a race to a place.

Short cuts reflect short-term thinking. And, like short-term thinking, they become handicaps sooner or later. They undercut and often destroy the very success we are trying to achieve.

Unfortunately, television and advertisements have

conditioned us to believe that life is supposed to be easy; that wealth is just minutes away; and that there's no problem that can't be solved in a 30-minute sitcom or a 30-second commercial. Then there are the TV gurus who preach that they can save us with their own homespun versions of quick fixes to wealth. It just isn't true. If it were, everyone would be doing it and everyone would be extremely wealthy.

Success takes time. I know. It used to be that I wanted everything to happen overnight. I didn't realize the seasoning effect that time has on the longevity of success. This is a lesson worth applying in our lives as a universal law. Let's forget short cuts and enjoy the process as well as the success it brings. Let's take the time and make the effort to travel the right road.

Remember:
- Don't short-change yourself.
- There are no short cuts to success.

Never Stop Starting

During one of the bleakest periods of World War II, Winston Churchill stood before the members of Great Britain's Parliament and made one of history's most memorable – and shortest – speeches. It consisted of seven words: "Never give up. Never, never give up."

The publisher, Malcolm Forbes, said the same thing: "Never, never, never, never give up." I like to say, "Never, never, never, never stop starting." Success is the never-ending process of refusing to give up.

History is filled with examples of men and women who have used this process to achieve extraordinary goals. Take Thomas Edison, for example. He failed more than 1,000 times to invent the electric light bulb. But he wouldn't give up. He failed and started over and failed and started over, and did this again and again and again until, after a thousand failures, he finally achieved a success that illuminated the world.

At any point along the way, Edison could have quit. But he didn't. He simply went back to the beginning and tried again, learning from what *wouldn't* work to find something that *would*.

When I lost everything, I had to start over. I had faced a crushing personal defeat. I could have quit. At times I desperately wanted to. But I knew I had to build something more solid and lasting than I had before.

In the process of starting over, I had to overcome my "enemy self" – my own weaknesses and fears and impatience – in order to become a person that deserved another shot at success.

My own personal tragedies were not life-threatening, but they *were* dramatic and life-changing. Perhaps you're having such problems in your own life at this time. If you are, I can relate. So can many others who have fought their way back. I know it's difficult, but no matter how hard it gets, I want you to know that *you can succeed!*

But you have to start today. And then start again tomorrow. And the next day.

We must move forward steadily, understanding that lasting success takes time. We must keep moving and not become discouraged. We can count on life to be difficult, but we can also expect success to smile upon us in return for our refusal to give up, and for our willingness to grit our teeth and start over. That's how it works.

If we falter or lose momentum, it's not the end. It's natural. When it happens, we should think of it as another chance to begin and start over.

The trick is to keep learning from our mistakes – to remember what caused us to falter and avoid it. We should look for all the positives we can find along the way. Above all, we must just "keep on keepin' on."

We hear of people ridiculing those that lose weight and then gain it all back and then some. But as long as these people refuse to give up and are willing to start over again, the battle is not lost. The only people who are lost and have failed are those who have decided that it is pointless for them to continue attempting to get out of the mire in which they exist.

Never forget: as long as we keep trying, we're still in the game.

Remember:
*   Never give up!
*   Keep starting over.

I Will. I Can.

It is important to incorporate the phrases "I will" and "I can" into our internal and spoken vocabulary, and to get rid of the words, "maybe," "if," "might," and "try." We should listen to ourselves when we speak to others and to ourselves and be constantly vigilant against those words.

The words we use are powerful. They influence us. When we say, "I'll try," rather than "I will," we're consciously and subconsciously setting ourselves up for the possibility of failure.

But when we say "I will" and "I can," we are positively affirming and confirming the things we're speaking or thinking about. The impact this has on our overall confidence, our attitude, and our success in achieving the very things we're discussing is astonishing. Why? Because our subconscious minds don't know the difference between what is real and what is vividly imagined.

When we say we "might," the message we give to ourselves and those who hear us say it is that there's a good possibility that we won't. Thus, we're setting ourselves up for failure again and again, and admitting it to others. Words like "maybe," "if," "might," and "try" are crutches that give us an escape clause – a way to wiggle out of our commitments.

A simple example of this is when people are asked if they are going to come to a party, and they say, "I'll try." That usually means they won't be there. But when they say, "I will" or "I can," the message is positive, one of commitment. It confirms to themselves and others that they definitely will do it. The power of these words is absolutely amazing!

Remember:
- I will. I can.

The Power of Living Right

When we follow life's fundamental moral laws and live as we know we should, we build up a reservoir of positive internal energy that will benefit us forever.

I believe we all have within ourselves a criteria for living, a map, a guideline, a set of rules that governs the way we feel about ourselves because of what we say, think, and do. I'm not referring to the rules of society, but rather to those that seem to have come with us when we were born – that innate road map of right and wrong that is a part of us. It has been called the "still, small voice" within us that guides us to be our best selves if we live according to what it tells us is true and right for us. Following that "voice" will enable us to move further and faster toward our Personal Best.

To get ahead and feel good about ourselves, we must first live according to the moral rules and ethics that we believe to be right. Second, we must give genuine, valuable service to others.

People are attracted to strength of character.

Sure, we can deceive some people with a carefully masked facade. But remember – that's a short cut. And short cuts undermine our ultimate, lasting success. We'll always run the risk of people "finding us out." We'll always need to find new people to scam. And we'll always have to look over our shoulders.

It's not worth it. By living in a way that is consistent with our principles, we will give people true value. This will move us quickly closer to enduring success. Best of all, our outward prosperity will be matched by inner happiness.

Remember:
• Exercise strength of character.

Don't Go Near The Edge

There's an old story about a stagecoach company that was looking for drivers. The owner set up interviews with three men for the job. These drivers were the best of the best.

The owner had each of them come into his office, one at a time, and asked them all the same question. The question was, "How close can you come to the edge of a cliff without going over?"

The first man responded arrogantly, "That's no problem for me. I can go full speed and get within twelve inches of the edge without going over."

The next man responded in like manner saying, "I just cut my speed back a little, but I can come within six inches of the edge without going over."

The third man answered quite differently saying, "I'd slow down and stay as far away as possible from the edge."

He got the job.

We don't need to live life on the edge all the time. We should stay away from the edge and avoid walking the line. Take it from me – it's not worth it. Why live with that extra stress and set ourselves up for a fall if we don't have to? Let's allow for a reasonable margin of safety in all we do in our lives.

Remember:
• 　　Don't push it over the edge.

Dealing With the Road Debris of Life

When I consult with people or speak to groups, I like to use the following analogy to illustrate the different ways people deal with choices and opportunities:

You are driving down the road one evening on your way home. It's late and there are no street lights on the road. You're tired and want to get home and go to bed. Suddenly, you see a twisted metal shelf unit in the middle of the road. What do you do?

Different people handle this type of situation in different ways. One person will swerve around it and continue driving home. Another will swerve around it and keep going, but will wonder whether someone else will not see it and hit it. Yet another person will react the same way, but will *almost* stop to move it off the road. Then there is the person who swerves around it, goes past it, stops, and goes back to throw it off the road. Another driver swerves around it, stops immediately, and throws it off the side of the road. The next person is paying attention, sees it before having to swerve, stops, and throws it off the road.

There is a remarkable difference between the person who swerves around the potentially dangerous road debris and continues home without thinking twice, and the person who sees it coming, and automatically stops without having to swerve and throws it out of the way. The former thinks only of himself and is happy that he or his car didn't get harmed. The latter is aware of what's going on around him, and of his responsibility to help others.

Many people who hear this example think that it has nothing to do with success and the ability to capitalize on opportunities. In reality, it has everything to do with these key issues. If we are so engrossed in ourselves and in what matters only to us, we will swerve around and pass by many potential opportunities. When we are concerned for others, we become more aware of what's happening around us, and are able to recognize opportunities – even business opportunities – that we would otherwise not see.

Remember:
- Develop an attitude of concern for everyone.

Are We Having Fun Yet?

Once we've started down the road that leads to personal transformation, it's important to be aware that the newness will eventually wear off. When this happens, we shouldn't be surprised if it starts to feel like *work*.

At first we felt tremendous excitement when we saw ourselves making real and important changes. But as we become used to making progress, the changes may seem more commonplace to us.

We mustn't lose sight of what is really happening. Instead, we should take time to take stock, reflect on how we're doing, and look at where we *are* compared to where we *were*. And we must never forget to give ourselves permission to feel pride in our accomplishments.

A great way to keep our perspective is to keep a journal. It doesn't have to be anything elaborate. We simply need to take some time – whether it's once a day or once a week – to write down our thoughts and impressions, record our goals, and keep track of our achievements. (More about journals later in this book.)

The main point is, we should never take our progress for granted just because we get used to it. Nor should we ever forget to pat ourselves on the back and enjoy the thrill of positive change.

Remember:
• Notice your progress.

No Problem!

Some people call life's undesirable events *problems*. Not me. I call them *challenges*.

So should you. It's simply a matter of perspective. Looking at a situation as a challenge rather than a problem immediately changes the way we think about it. It becomes easier to handle and more exciting to overcome. A realistic understanding of challenges can make all the difference in our attitude and our ultimate success.

Challenges help build character. They are a necessary part of life. They make us strong. If everything were easy to accomplish, everyone would be wealthy and successful. The extraordinary would become commonplace.

If we don't have any challenges, that's when we should start to worry! The only people who don't have challenges are those who aren't trying to grow.

Did you ever hear of anyone who waited to take a road trip until all the lights were green and all the traffic was out of the way? Of course not. But that's the approach many people take when it comes to personal change. They want to be sure everything will work out before they even start.

We can't anticipate everything that will come along. Even if we could, we'd be wasting a lot of time worrying. Have you ever noticed how worrying about something is much harder than simply dealing with it when it comes along? Besides, many of the things that we see from a distance as "problems" will resolve themselves before we ever have to confront them directly.

Someone once said, "Whenever I look up the road and see ten problems coming in my direction, I don't ever worry. By the time they have gotten to me, five have run off the road, three have broken down, and at least one of the other two have stopped with a flat tire."

But what about the problems that *do* reach us? No problem! Simply rename them. Remember? The moment we call a problem a challenge, it ceases to be a problem.

So you see, there really are no problems. There are only challenges that strengthen us and make us better. Consider the difference between the pine tree and the oak tree. The roots of pine trees are shallow. They don't sink deep into the soil. The roots of oak trees, on the other hand, plunge deep into the soil. The harder the wind blows, the deeper into the ground they send their roots. In short, they respond to this challenge by becoming stronger. And so they stand the test of time.

If we want to become mighty oaks, we should welcome rather than lament the winds of challenge that surely blow through our lives. It is only these trials and adversities that will drive our shallow roots deep into the soil of character and fortitude, transforming us from vulnerable pines to oaks of strength.

So the next time a gale-force wind tries to knock us down, let's remember this important phrase: "No Problem!"

Remember:
- Strength comes through challenges.

Can We Be Taught?

Think about that question for a moment. Many very intelligent people can learn ... but can they be taught?

A major requirement for making money, achieving happiness, or getting whatever it is we want out of life, is to be *teachable*.

Being teachable is to accept that we don't know it all, and to be willing to absorb incoming knowledge and information. When we are teachable, we will listen to and learn from others who have gone down the path we want to follow – people who have experienced life and are willing to share what they've learned with us.

Opening our minds to life's lessons will help us learn and grow on a daily basis. We must allow our minds to accept information, purely and impartially, and work to combat rigid thinking and narrow-mindedness. We must never shut the lid on our minds and put a lock on them.

Think of life as an extended seminar – a teaching and learning process.

Some years ago I was blessed to have a wonderful and powerful mentor. This man typically wouldn't hire people over the age of 25 to work in his sales and marketing business. He reasoned that by the time they were 25 they had already learned to sell a certain way and were usually unwilling to change.

I've found this to be generally true. We all tend to get set in our ways, and it's uncomfortable and awkward to change – sometimes downright painful. That's why so many people resist being taught something new. When we learn something, we might have to make changes. And changes can be very uncomfortable. Yet we grow and progress when we change.

People who are trying to kick drug or alcohol habits must

first admit that they need help. Only when their minds are open to counsel can they move forward. Similarly, people who are trying to learn must first admit that they need help in the form of knowledge or information. Only then will they open their minds and be teachable.

Teachability demands humility. Sometimes it's difficult to swallow our pride and admit that there's something we don't know. But at least we have the benefit of knowing that we're in good company. After earning a reputation for his vast knowledge, Socrates admitted that the only thing that made him smarter than the next person was that he knew enough to know that he knew virtually nothing.

It's like the old saying: "The more you know, the more you realize you *don't* know." It's true. The more we learn, the clearer our thinking becomes, and the more our minds open to the vastness of knowledge that exists in all aspects of life. As we learn more, our humility should grow, because we should realize that there is so much more out there to learn. When we admit this to ourselves, we become even more teachable.

Teachable people have a thirst for knowledge. Books and wisdom become their food. They don't waste their time – and their minds – on television and mindless reading. They devour any information they can get that propels them closer to their goals, whatever those objectives happen to be.

What does this say about people who walk around as if they know it all? They are merely proclaiming to the world that they are ignorant and unenlightened.

When I hire people to work with me, I usually take their resumes and turn them face down on my desk. As far as I'm concerned, I don't care if they have seven Ph.D.s or a list of credentials that fills a book. What I care about is how teachable they are, and what kind of people they are. I want to know if I'll be able to teach them my system – my way of doing things – or if they are going to think that their way is the best? Will they want to learn, or will they want to feel superior?

I once interviewed a gentleman in his 50s for a job. He had

never made over $30,000 a year. He was in commercial real estate, selling shopping centers. It didn't bother me that he hadn't made more money. In fact, that made me hope that he might be more teachable than most people. But he wasn't. He came across like he knew everything. He later called and asked me why I didn't hire him. I was glad he called. I told him he gave me the impression that he knew it all. I explained that I needed people who are teachable. He realized I was right and said goodbye.

Teachability is the foundation of growth. In order to grow, we must learn; in order to learn, we must be willing to be taught; and in order to be taught, we must put our minds in a "growth mode" and admit that we don't know everything. When we're willing to admit that, and to let ourselves be taught, we're ready to take a giant leap forward.

Remember:
- Open your mind.
- Always be teachable.

Which Way?

Some people think that asking questions is a sign of stupidity. What they don't realize is that the opposite is true: individuals that ask questions are actually demonstrating their willingness to be taught and to learn, which is a sign of intelligence. They are saying, "I'm teachable. I want to know." Consequently, they learn things that others don't, or learn things faster.

An example of asking questions is asking directions when you're driving around looking for an address. Some people would rather drive around lost for hours than stop to ask directions. (Men are more guilty of this than women.) My dad would drive around for hours, it seemed, without asking directions because he didn't think he needed anyone's help. He thought he could find it himself.

If we don't know how to get somewhere, ask for directions! Stop and ask, then drive a little further and confirm the directions with someone else. By taking this advice – we'll save ourselves precious time and eliminate a lot of unnecessary frustration.

Remember:
- Ask questions.

Loosen Up!

A medical authority said, "The time is coming when vacations will be given as prescriptions; when doctors ... will discern the subtle causes of our deep-seated maladies, and will lead us gently back to the carefree playtime of childhood."

Look at yourself in the mirror. Do you see someone that people will look at and say, "Man, that guy needs to loosen up!"

Relax. Lighten up. Let the walls down.

Remember, we're all human. Too many people are uptight and stiff. They walk around like time bombs. Whatever gnaws at us, we should let it go, keep perspective, and have some fun.

It's easy to get too serious about life. I know there are millions of reasons and good excuses to feel negative, over-burdened, and serious. But we don't have to feel that way if we don't want to. *We* are in charge of how we feel!

Here's a trick: if we find that we're taking ourselves too seriously, we should spend some time around children. They'll teach us what's important and how to look at life with a sparkle in our eyes again.

Speaking of children, Art Linkletter said, "It's a world where nothing is predictable and nothing is commonplace because everything is fresh and unexpected and new ..."

Willie Snow Ethridge tells a story about his grandchildren. They had been asked whether they were afraid of lightning. "No!" answered one of them, sounding a bit shocked at the idea. "The lightning just makes little mornings out of the night."

Seeing the world through a child's eyes will change our perspectives immediately. It's a great way to loosen up.

Remember:
- Relax and *Change!*

Taking Care of the "Little" Things

Surveys show that only 1 percent of the people in this country are financially successful by today's standards and definitions. What is it that this successful 1 percent do that the other 99 percent don't?

I believe that the answer lies in what we would call the "small" things.

What might seem to be a small thing can yield very big results. A race horse or professional athlete can win a national championship by a very small fraction of a second. But the difference between the winnings of the champion and the second-place competitor is usually a very large amount of money – tens, even hundreds of thousand of dollars! Did the champion try that much harder or do that much better than the runner-up? No! The difference in life is found in the small things – the little things that no one pays much attention to except the champions.

By doing the small things, we can place ourselves in that top 1 percent category of truly successful people. Here are some of those little things we can do that will pay huge dividends:

- Push harder when we practice.
- Read books when others say there is no time.
- Converse with people openly when others are holding things in.
- Take the time to exercise regularly when others say they don't have enough time.
- Keep ourselves clean and well groomed when others rush through their personal hygiene chores as if they weren't important.
- Listen to educational or motivational tapes in the car when others are listening to blaring music or mindless chatter.

- Send "thank you" cards and notes to friends and business associates instead of just closing the deal and forgetting about them.
- Make phone calls and pay compliments instead of passing over these acts of kindness, thinking they don't matter.
- Volunteer our service and skills to the unfortunate, while others simply donate money because they think they are too busy.
- Thank our Heavenly Father for all that we have, rather than thinking we did it all on our own.
- Call family members to express our love without expecting it in return.
- Hug our spouses and children frequently, even though we may not have been hugged as a child.
- Love even when we are not loved.
- Give even when we feel we are in need.

These may appear to be small, insignificant things. But small things grow into big things. Let's remember that two ships traveling side by side at the beginning of a voyage will end up on opposite sides of the world if one moves to the right just one degree! Let's put this same principle to work in our own lives and join that successful 1 percent.

Remember:
- Do the little things that lead to success.

Key 2:

REMOVING MIND CLUTTER

Develop Mental Focus

When reporters or talk show hosts interview me, they often ask about the mental aspects of success. The subject of focus is usually brought up. "How important is it to have mental focus in order to succeed?" is a common question.

In response, I explain that I travel across the United States and abroad, working with individuals and companies, and one of the biggest problems I encounter – especially with individuals – is that they try to do too many things at the same time. Many of these people work full-time at regular jobs, try to do real estate on the side, work some multilevel program during the evening hours, and sometimes do something "extra" on the weekends.

There is no way that these people are ever going to be truly successful by being involved in so many unrelated business activities at once. Why? Because they lack focus.

If we want to have prosperity and fulfillment in our lives, we need to focus on *one* activity and dedicate ourselves to it completely and passionately. We should give it everything we've got. Then, and only then, will we be able to reap the rewards it offers. This will happen because we will be totally – not just partially – involved.

People often defend their involvement in so many different activities by pointing to the fact that they are staying very busy. So what? Too many people confuse being busy with being productive. They think that in order to be successful they must stay busy, and in order to stay busy they must be involved in several projects at one time. They feel that they must be getting somewhere because they're always in motion. Wrong!

I've seen too many people get addicted to constantly starting one job after another simply because they feel successful by occupying their time with a lot of things to do. The trouble is, they rarely finish anything, and never get anywhere because they aren't focused.

We all should take a personal inventory of the activities in which we're involved that are supposed to help us make money. We should make a list, and next to each entry, make a note of how much of our time is dedicated to that activity. Next, we write down how much money we make from each activity. (It's important to be honest – no pretending and no projections.)

When I have my clients go through this exercise, the excuse I often hear is "Well, I'm just getting started." Come on! For two years?

Chances are, once we've made this list, we'll see that some of the things we're doing to make money aren't accomplishing their objective. We should drop them, and commit the time and effort we've been wasting on them to the one, single activity that will make it happen for us.

Until we focus on what we want and put ourselves into it, completely, we'll never know what our true potential really is. Many people have the right ideas and even the correct motivations and goals, but they lack focus. What a tragedy it is that so many men and women go to the grave without ever putting their potential to the test!

Let me make an important point here. I'm not saying that we should devote all our time and effort to one single thing. That would be disastrous. We can't ignore all the other aspects of our lives that are important and make us well-rounded individuals. But at the same time, we mustn't let our energies become so diluted by "everything" that we don't have enough juice to do that "something" that will make a real difference.

The trick is to focus on one thing at a time. When we're working, we should focus intensely on what we're doing. When we're paying bills, we need to focus on that and get it quickly and accurately out of the way.

When Michelangelo was painting the ceiling of the Sistine Chapel, he still had to eat, sleep, take care of his bodily functions, attend to the personal relationships in his life, pay bills, and so on. Yet when he was working, he *focused* on his monumental project with a fiery intensity. If he hadn't, it would not have been the masterpiece it is. If his thoughts had been on what he was going to eat that night, or on whether to sign up as a distributor in the multilevel marketing company his brother-in-law was pressing him to join, he would have been just another Italian artist whose name and works would soon have faded into obscurity.

Developing mental focus isn't easy. It takes practice. We must train our minds to focus precisely on a goal. When we're involved in something, we need to "compartmentalize" the other aspects of our lives and put them "on the shelf" so that thinking about them won't dilute or derail what we're trying to accomplish at the moment.

In reality, our productivity is directly related to our ability to focus, not to our capacity to juggle numerous tasks at once. While juggling a variety of tasks may give us the illusion of being productive, we're probably just spinning our wheels. That isn't successful behavior. It's counterproductive.

A story about Albert Einstein gives us a striking example of focus. Walking down a street one day, Einstein came upon a friend and became engrossed in conversation. He focused so intently on the dialogue that as they parted he had to ask his friend which direction he had been walking when they met.

We can train our minds to concentrate on one thing at a time, and one thing only.

One way to practice this is to read something and focus on it completely. As we read, we should observe how many times our thoughts drift off to something else. If we sail off to another thought, we then have to begin reading again. We should try this for 10 or 15 minutes. For many of us, this is a real challenge at first. The fact is, most people find it very difficult to focus until they train themselves to do so.

A man once bet a friend that he couldn't repeat the *Lord's Prayer* without his mind wandering. If he could, he'd win a horse. The friend said, "That's easy – you're on!" He began: "Our Father who art in heaven, hallowed be thy name.... Say, will you throw in the saddle, too?"

It's normal to drift. However, we want to improve our skills beyond what is normal, or natural. This is what this book is all about.

We need to work on this until we can become intensely focused on what we're doing without consciously trying.

When we develop this ability, we'll be like the magnifying glass that can focus a few square inches of sunlight into a dot of such intense heat that it can burn holes through wood.

Imagine what we could do with that kind of power!

Remember:
- Streamline your activities.
- Develop focus.

Mastering Ourselves

A program director for a large corporation wanted to hire a motivational speaker to conduct workshops for the company. He was given a list of potential candidates, and he went to hear each of the best candidates speak. It came down to two qualified, talented individuals.

After listening to each of them one more time, the decision was easily made. One of the speakers swore in his presentation. The program director immediately crossed off his name.

When that speaker called to ask why he wasn't chosen, the program director told him. The speaker said he could delete the bad language from his presentation. But the program director said that he wanted someone that didn't need to take it out of his program at all. He wanted the kind of person that wouldn't have included it in the first place. He wanted someone who had mastered himself enough to keep his language on a higher plane.

It was a question of self-control.

Let's master ourselves! This is the ultimate goal.

Our ability to build and maintain restraint, discipline, and self-control is *power!*

It has been said that everyone's number one goal should be the pursuit of self-control. Brian Tracy, a personal development trainer, calls self-control the "master skill."

If we can control ourselves, we can control anything. If we have not mastered ourselves, how can we expect to have power over the many elements of our personal and business lives that seem so elusive?

When we are in control of ourselves, we are in a position to act, rather than being constantly acted upon. If we have ourselves in check, we will be able to focus on objectives and streamline our lives with clarity and direction.

In my book, *Rags to Riches to Rags to Riches*, I relate a story from the movie, *Billy Jack*. When Billy Jack told his master that he was ready to become a master himself, he suddenly found himself in a dream. He was in a tavern, where a bully started getting obnoxious and rough with some Native American women. When Billy told the man to leave the women alone, the man shoved him, then slapped him across the face. This enraged Billy, who quickly dropped the bully to the ground with a couple of well-placed punches and kicks.

After the dream, Billy's master asked him how he fared. Billy responded that he did fine – the guy made him mad and he defended the woman. The master asked Billy how he made him mad, and Billy said that he had slapped him across the face.

The master then told Billy to slap *him*. Billy said no, but on his master's insistence, finally obeyed. The master stood tall and straight, his arms calmly at his sides. "You can't make me mad," he said. "You can't make me anything. *I* choose."

This helped Billy realize that he had allowed someone else to control him by making him mad, and had blamed his behavior on someone else's actions. He realized that until he could learn to control himself, he wasn't ready to be a master.

What a challenge it is to try to control and overcome our anger, our desires to eat and drink too much, or the temptation to swear or criticize! Gaining self-control is the challenge of all challenges. But I know that if we learn to control ourselves, we'll be true successes.

Unfortunately, there's no shortage of habits, weaknesses, and cravings that fight to control us. Many people are controlled by cigarettes, alcohol, bad language, sexuality, cravings for food, and so on. These are the more obvious and visible controllers. But there are many other would-be controllers that are not so visible: negative-thinking, television, procrastination, sarcasm, apathy, and laziness, to name a few.

Some of the most dangerous and damaging controllers we face as human beings, in my opinion, are improper behavior, impure thoughts and actions, and other violations of our personal moral and ethical codes. These are particularly devastating because they tear down our self-confidence.

Inside all of us exists a subconscious mind. This is the place where we cannot hide. If we are doing something we shouldn't and think we are getting away with it because we haven't been caught, we've already placed ourselves in the strongest of prisons. We've stolen the potential from our lives that exists if we're true to ourselves and our knowledge of good and evil.

I believe that we can only reach our full potential if we live our lives according to the written and unwritten rules that we know should govern all people.

By adhering to these principles, we free ourselves from the internal turmoil that is felt by so many of our fellow human beings. In business, many deals are consummated because someone says, "Well, I just feel good about him." When people "feel good" about someone, it is usually because that person feels good about himself or herself. And that comes when people live the way they know they ought to. They experience *Change!*

Because I spend a lot of my time consulting with people who are striving to achieve wealth, I want to make special mention of financial self-control and the lack of it.

The natural tendency when we start doing well is to want to flaunt it and show it to the world. Typically this happens when we make good money for the first time and we find ourselves with cash and the desire for "things."

Just because we suddenly find ourselves in the financial position to spend money on an expensive car does not mean that we need to. Why not take a portion of the money we make and put it in the bank? It will give us a sense of power. In fact, it *will* give us power.

Spending money on an expensive car is the typical thing people who are new to money do. They have an almost juvenile approach to finance. It's as if they're saying, "I've got it and I want to show it." Believe me, most people see right through that.

When I heard that Sam Walton and Bill Marriott drove

standard, middle-income automobiles, I wondered why. Then I figured it out: they had nothing to prove to anyone. They were confident in themselves and comfortable with where they were and who they were. That's a wonderful place to be – to be able to purchase anything you need, yet to remain conservative. That is truly mastering yourself. And it's vital to long term, stable success.

This principle of having the power to do something and then not doing it applies to everything in life – not just money.

For example, let's say someone gives us a hard time and challenges us to a fight. Let's also say that we're black belts in karate, and we know we have the skills and the power to beat the bully to a pulp. But we exercise our self-control, and instead of fighting, we respectfully decline. We have nothing to prove to anyone. We have no desire to take advantage of some sorry soul who doesn't have his act together. We know that the most powerful person is the one who controls the situation, and the one who controls the situation is the one who exercises self-control. By declining to fight, we win on both counts.

Once we achieve total self-control, we unlock our greatest potential and experience true *Change!*

Remember:
- Master yourself.
- Self-control is power.

Go For It!

I wrestled in high school with a guy named Phil Lauro. He taught me the meaning of the term "go for it."

Every day, Phil wrestled as if his life depended on it. When people visited our practices, they always asked if he was getting ready for the national tournaments. He wasn't. He just put everything he had into it. Always.

Fortunately for me, Phil was my wrestling partner. I had the opportunity to wrestle with him every day. My season turned out to be an excellent one largely because I adopted Phil's philosophy. I won 14 matches with 13 pins. (A "pin" is to wrestling what a knockout is to boxing.) I didn't lose a match.

It was an important lesson for me: "Go for it!" Always. Every day. In every way.

We should apply this principle to every aspect of our lives, universally. I believe we'll be surprised by the results.

Remember:
- Go for it every minute of every day.

Positivism is Contagious

I used to run along a trail in Atlanta at six o'clock in the morning. During the winter months the temperature would drop to a chilly 20 to 30 degrees. It would have been easy to turn my thoughts inward and shut out the world and the cold.

But I didn't. I said hello to the people I met as I ran. When I first started doing this, people thought I was crazy. After all, nobody says hello at six in the morning in the dark, right? So they spoke to me only if I spoke to them first, out of obligation.

But things changed. Several people started greeting me before I ever got a chance to say hello to them. It was as if I created a little group of friends on the trail. Today, these people are probably happier and much more friendly, and I feel good because of it.

This is proof to me that a positive person has a positive effect on the people around him or her. Positivism is definitely contagious.

The same principle applies universally. Have you ever noticed at the supermarket check-out counters how some checkers never speak to you, and sometimes never even look at you?

I've noticed it. And I feel a responsibility – because I've been so blessed – to try my best to make these people's days brighter by saying something positive. Then, hopefully, they will say something nice to the next person in return. These people probably don't even know they're being rude and unkind, and a little shot of positivism is all they usually need to brighten up. Say something nice. Compliment their hair style or their clothes. People aren't used to that kind of treatment. It will usually throw them off balance just long enough to let a little positivism creep in, and bring a smile to their faces.

Some people, however, need a dose of stronger medicine. Once I was in line at a grocery store and the checker was so unbelievably rude to the elderly woman in front of me that I had to say something. It was not a situation that called for a nice, cheerful word. It demanded directness, and I was direct.

Sometimes we have to stand up for what we believe and say what we feel is needed. But when we do, it's important that we do it in a positive way. We can be direct and forceful and still be positive.

The point is not to go around telling everyone what we think, but rather to take on the responsibility of helping people out whenever and wherever we can. Whether that requires a direct, strong comment, or (in most cases) just a positive word or compliment, we will be making a difference ... a *positive* difference.

Remember:
- Exude positivism. Start an epidemic!

Visualize Success

The process and exercise of visualization helps our goals become realities.

We need to spend time visualizing ourselves in the circumstances we want to be in, or in possession of what we want, or as the type of person we want to be.

We should do more than just put up signs, pictures, and inspirational sayings. We should actually picture ourselves already *there*. The more we're able to visualize the achievement of our goals, and the more precise we make that visualization, the more that vision will help us arrive at that goal.

For instance, let's say we want a particular sports car. Why stop at simply putting a picture of it up on the wall? That's not "six-figure thinking." Instead, we should go take a test drive, then have our picture taken next to it, in it, in our driveway, and driving it. We should blow the photos up and put them in our offices or our bedrooms where we'll see them every day. How about making a poster out of one of them, and then framing it? How about visualizing ourselves driving that shiny new car to friends' homes, sporting events, and social functions?

It's amazing what these exercises will do for our subconscious minds as we work to achieve our goals.

Do we want a specific house in a certain neighborhood? Then we should take a picture of it with us on the porch. We should visit it, talk to the neighbors, walk the neighborhood. We'll start to feel like we belong.

If we want to be wealthy, we need to act that way. We need to spend time where the wealthy congregate, and associate ourselves with them. We should frequent their sporting events, parties, and cultural events. This may seem difficult at first, but we'll start to think of ways to go to racquet clubs, golf courses, restaurants, and charity events.

We all remember the feeling when we first entered grade school or high school – that feeling of "not belonging," of not being one of "them." The best way to start to become one of them is to walk where they walk. This helps to make it more real to us.

This intense visualization process imprints our goals firmly on our subconscious minds, and in fact "tricks" our subconscious into believing that what we are visualizing has already happened.

Sounds like magic, doesn't it? But it's not. It is a widely acknowledged psychological truth. *Our subconscious minds can't distinguish between reality and intensely visualized fantasy.*

Once our subconscious minds believe that something is real, we will then begin to see real magic in our lives. Our powerful subconscious minds will work overtime to make our goals come true. We will begin to make the kinds of decisions a person with a big house makes. We will begin to act the way a wealthy person acts. Soon, outward realities will begin to conform to our subconscious realities, and we'll be where and whom we want to be, and have what we want to have.

A vacation is a perfect example of first creating something in our minds, then bringing it to life. Everything happens in our minds before it becomes a reality, and then we go to work to make it a physical reality. Before we leave on our vacations, we first decide to go. We make all the plans in our heads first. We visualize where we want to travel, what it looks and feels like, what we'll be doing, how much money we'll spend, how long we'll be gone, and so on.

We do all this before anything actually takes place. We "live" the vacation mentally, before ever experiencing it physically.

I want us all to start using this same process with our goals. We should picture them happening first – just like our vacations. We should see our goals occurring in our minds first, and in reality second. This works!

The more fully we realize how our future is shaped by the way we look at and think about things, the more we'll understand how powerful our minds are in changing our present situations. The goals we have in our lives today, much like our vacations, will never come to fruition unless we first spend time entertaining those ideas, mentally – visualizing them in detail.

Great religious leaders have told us for thousands of years that we create our own realities through our beliefs. Visualization is merely belief with a visual aspect. Through visualization, we *do* create our realities.

The trouble is, too many of us visualize negative things – like the kid who goes up to bat saying, "I know I'm going to strike out!" We tend to go up to the bat in business or in our personal affairs saying, "I know I'll strike out!" With that kind of visualization, we generally do.

Let's not fall into that trap. Let's make sure that what we are visualizing is positive. It's up to us! *What we visualize – whether it's positive or negative – is completely within our control.* We need to make sure that our minds are clear and focused and positive, or else we will be our own demise. If we visualize good, positive things for ourselves, they will become realities sooner than we might think.

Remember:
* Visualize every detail.
* Use your mind and make your dreams real.

Organizing and Uncluttering Our Minds

I've found the use of "TO DO" lists to be a powerful tool.

You'd be amazed how much more we can accomplish in a day if we write things down and tackle one thing at a time from our lists.

Most people use "TO DO" lists when they go to the grocery store or on a trip to make sure they don't forget anything. Or they make a list of jobs that need to be done over a weekend. But we should use these lists *all* the time – especially in our work. If shopping and trips and weekend jobs are important, how much more important are our business affairs?

I keep a list every day. The list shows me quickly what I need to do and lets me easily prioritize, so that I can accomplish the most important items first. One side benefit to working off my list is that as I accomplish each task I get to cross it off. That serves as an immediate reward, and gives me a real sense of accomplishment.

I keep a dated "TO DO" list. As I finish each item, I mark it off. If I need to call people, I have their names and phone numbers in one place. If I call them and they aren't home, I write "NH" for "not home" next to the note. If I leave a message for them with another person, or on an answering machine, I write "LM" for "left message." If they're going to call me back, I jot down "CM" for "calling me."

This rids my mind of all the little bits and pieces of information that clutter up my head. Most people's minds are so full of mental "TO DO" notes that they have no room left for creativity, higher-level thinking, or new ideas. With a brain-full of "Post-It" notes stuffed into their heads, how can they concentrate their attention on the important work that requires focus?

Albert Einstein – one of my personal favorites – once admitted that he didn't know his own telephone number. When asked how such an intelligent man could not remember his own number, he responded, "Why should I memorize something I can look up?"

Good point, Einstein! Why should you? Why should *we*? This story put me on a crusade to empty my mind of the facts that can be reduced to paper, and help the people I teach and consult do the same. If we are ever going to use the most powerful resource we possess (our minds) in a way that truly utilizes their strength, we must not clutter them with the mundane, incidental thoughts and concerns that can so easily be committed to paper and then put aside.

For example, instead of trying to remember all day long to go to the dry cleaners after work, why not simply make a note on a "TO DO" list? Some people even write a note and tape it to the dashboard of their cars. Then at the end of the day when they get in their cars to go home, they see it and do it.

Whatever technique works best for us, the point is to avoid having to mentally inventory that information so we don't forget. To me, that is a terrible waste of mental powers. It also leads to forgetting a lot of important things that we should do, and losing important ideas and concepts that suddenly come to us, only to be forgotten because we didn't write them down.

I believe our minds have differing capacities to think, to store information, and to create. I don't know what yours is, but I know that by emptying our minds of facts that we can write down on paper, we are increasing our odds of coming up with something creative. And creativity – originating a new idea or an improvement on an old idea – is precisely what success is built upon. Many investors admit that they do not find deals; rather, they *create* them from the same information that everyone else has at their fingertips. "TO DO" lists will unclutter our minds to work in the same way.

It is proven that these lists will save us money. People going in to shop with a list of items to buy are in the stores shorter periods of time and spend less money. People who keep lists of tasks are able to be much more efficient during business hours and in their personal lives by following their lists, as opposed to just waking up and saying, "Well, what should I do today?"

There are several tips that can make this use of lists more effective. One is to make sure that we use one single list for the day rather than many scattered, pieced-together lists and "Post-It" notes. That is as ineffective as having no list at all.

Also, we need to make list-making a habit, and to be consistent in using and executing our lists.

Another important tip is to always tackle the most difficult task first, or the one we dislike the most. If we avoid the "tough" tasks, they will be burdens on our minds all day. We need to get them out of the way first, and the rest of the day will seem easy!

This is critical: we should include in our lists the truly important things in our lives, like reading a self-improvement book, or taking a daughter to lunch on her birthday. Let's not let what is *urgent* bully us into not doing what is *important*. We need to make appointments with ourselves to do the important things. We should actually mark off time slots on our calendars to exercise, meditate, and take care of domestic activities.

We're accustomed to doing this for meetings, projects, and other work-related events because we want to make sure they happen. Why? They're important. Well, *we are important too!*

A "Turbo" is a great way to organize ourselves and keep track of the many aspects of our lives and our many projects, thoughts, ideas, and TO DOs without needlessly cluttering our minds. These are small, three-ring binders with several sections separated by tabs. We can customize the sections to meet our needs and preferences. I have TO DO sections for today, next week, and next month, plus sections for the specific projects and books I'm working on.

I also carry a microcassette recorder at all times. I find it especially helpful when I'm in the car and I remember something or get an idea or sudden inspiration. It has been proven that if we don't capture on paper or a tape the ideas that come to us, they won't come to us as frequently, and maybe not at all.

One final tip about "TO DO" lists: When we're in traffic driving and we have an important thought that should go on our lists (or even an idea worth remembering), it's difficult to pull over to write it down, and dangerous to do so while we're driving. One excellent idea is to get a microcassette recorder and record these thoughts on tape when we can't put them on paper. Then, later, we can transfer the notes to our lists. Microcassette recorders cost only about $30 or so, and many models are small enough to keep in a pocket. They become invaluable once we get used to using them. Our minds will be freer to be creative – even when we can't write something down – because we know we can easily record our next important reminder or million-dollar idea.

Remember:

- Use "TO DO" lists always.
- Do the most difficult task first.

Balance

My parents both died when they were 58. Why? There were several reasons. They didn't eat right, they didn't exercise, and they didn't take the proper precautions with their habits. Their lives were not balanced.

Without the proper mental, spiritual, physical, educational, family, social and financial balance, our lives will eventually attempt to correct the situation. This attempt often manifests itself in the form of ulcers, heart attacks, divorce, financial problems, and so on. Maintaining proper balance is crucial not only to our success, but to our very survival.

Balance is vital!

One of our first and most important goals should be to achieve and maintain balance between all the different facets of our lives. Let's not be among those people who overemphasize one area of their lives while neglecting other areas. If we work out at a gym for several hours every day, we'll have no extra time for anything else and will very likely begin to neglect our family duties, career opportunities, and the other things we shouldn't neglect. If we go to work early and stay late every day, we'll sacrifice our personal lives. Everything else will be left waiting in line.

One of the most common imbalances is "workaholism." Financial success is the goal of many people, but workaholics don't realize (or perhaps they refuse to recognize) that working non-stop at the office is not going to get them there any faster. It may seem logical that productivity will increase proportionately to the amount of time a person works, but this has been proven to be dead wrong.

If we don't eat a properly balanced diet, some part of our bodies or physiological systems will sooner or later suffer for it.

Similarly, if we don't balance our activities, we will eventually incur permanent damage in one or more areas of our lives.

It's a good idea to make a list of the various facets of our lives, prioritize them, and ask ourselves if each facet is getting an appropriate share of our time and efforts. If not, we need to make adjustments. And we must always remember that every choice we make has a price, so we need to try to be sure we're making the best choices.

Wouldn't it be worth the effort to start our lives over right now and begin to cultivate and maintain a healthy balance? Or do we want to let ourselves get sick, go broke, lose our families and friends, or die just when we're starting to finally understand what life is all about?

It's so easy to get caught up in our work or other activities and put our health, family, and everything else on the back burner. It's so easy to lose track of the things that mean the most in life!

While balance is very easy to lose, it certainly isn't easy to achieve or regain. Generally speaking, the way to bring balance into your life is to do lots of different kinds of things every day, and refrain from overindulging in any one area, or neglecting any area.

Here are a few specific suggestions to create balance:

- Read for 15 minutes a day.
- Exercise for 30 minutes a day.
- Take your spouse on a date at least once a week.
- Each week, do something special with one of your children (one at a time) on a rotating basis.
- Read scriptures or religious materials for ten minutes a day.
- Let your mind relax for 15 to 30 minutes a day.
- Write a letter to a family member; call a friend; talk to an acquaintance; or strike up a conversation with a stranger each day.
- Try a new hobby.

Let's remember to treat all aspects of our lives with the

importance they deserve. Many of them will not wait until we "get around to it," or until the time is better.

Whatever our situation is today, *now* is the best time to focus on balance ... before it's too late.

Remember:
- Develop and maintain balance in your life.

Don't Kick Me There – It Hurts!

When I give all-day seminars on human and personal development, there's an exercise I make everyone do. I learned it years ago. It helped me to become more aware of an aspect of life that can become easily unbalanced. Let's do it right now.

Take out a clean piece of paper with nothing written on it. Place it in front of you on a table. Now, get a pen and write the following in big letters that fill the page: E G O.

Okay? Put your pen down and raise the piece of paper over your head. Now, tear it in half and throw it up in the air.

What did you just do? Stop and think about it for a moment. What you did was literally tear up your "ego." It may seem silly now, but this is exactly what we all need to do in order to begin to change our lives.

Whether we believe it or not, tearing up our egos will open our lives to unbelievable new opportunities. In fact, I tell my audiences that they put $100,000 in their pockets just by tearing up that little piece of paper. By that, I mean that they will do better in every facet of their lives, including their businesses or careers, if they don't let their egos get in the way. People don't like to do business with people who are "into themselves." People like confidence – not cockiness and conceit. People who are conceited come across as jerks and snobs. They put others off. If we can tear our egos up and genuinely care about others, they will be drawn to us, and we will be more successful.

I once heard a little saying that goes: "Conceit is a disease that makes everyone sick except the person who has it." People who are in love with themselves have no idea how many opportunities they are losing because of their self-centered relationship.

I have met many people that I would never do business

with because they think they are better than those around them. You know the type. Have you ever gone to a store, and the owner or salesperson thought he was great and acted like you were a nobody? Chances are, you decided to go farther away from your home to another store where the owner was happy to have your business, greeted you with a smile, and gave you respect – someone who treated you as a valued, important person; someone who knew you were his lifeblood and knew that without people like you and me, he would have no business.

This type of business person gets *my* business every time. I will pay more and drive out of my way to patronize people like that. I refuse to pay my money to someone who does not treat me right because of an ego that may be inflated or out of balance.

I've turned down numerous consulting requests because of the way people have come across on the phone. They gave an image of being already too successful to be on this planet – acting like we all should be honored to know them and be in their presence. These people will never do business with me. I would rather lose the business than work with someone that I don't like or respect.

One of my corporate clients referred me to a company that was experiencing an average of 25 percent growth per year. The general manager said, "What do I need you for? We're already at the top!" I replied, "What makes you think you can't grow 25 percent *per month* instead of per year?"

No one wants to know that we think of ourselves as great or superior. If we feel that way, we need to fix it, and adjust our perspectives. We are just human beings. We all came from the same place. Yes, some of us may be doing better financially than others and may have positions of prominence at this moment in time. But that is no reason to walk around acting like "gods." No one appreciates that kind of attitude, and most people will go out of their way to avoid any contact with that type of person.

It's wonderful to have a healthy confidence in our abilities. But we should never let our egos run away with us. No one wants to be associated or do business with egotists. If we have egos that get in our way, we'll miss out on some of the best things in life because of it. If we feel that we are "above" our fellow men, we need to do the exercise I just described regularly: tear up our egos again and again, and bring ourselves back down to earth.

Remember:

•   Deflating your ego will inflate your success.

Key 3:

BREAKING OUT OF THE COMFORT ZONE

The Personal Roots
of Business Success

I've consulted one-on-one with many hundreds of clients over the years. I've gotten to know these people quite well, both on a personal and business level, and one thing I've found that has held true with virtually all of them is that their business lives – their careers – are never completely successful if their personal lives are not successful.

This realization had led me to what I believe is a universal principle: *We can't be our best professionally until we're "100 percent" in our personal lives.*

I've known people who need to lose weight, people who need to quit smoking, people who need to straighten out a close relationship ... people who need to "fix" some situation or another in their personal lives. Invariably, the personal challenges they face hold them back in their business or professional pursuits.

Personal problems that need fixing are like mineral build-ups in drain pipes. The more these problems build up, the more they "clog up" our chances of business success. If we ignore them, they gradually choke off the flow of success through our lives.

If one or more personal challenges are facing us, take action. Maybe they're mild situations that only need Draino. Or perhaps they're serious blockages that we can only clear up with a good Roto-Rooter job.

Whatever it takes, do it! Get started ... and get going today! Once we get our personal lives flowing smoothly and freely, we'll be surprised what will happen to our business lives.

Remember:
- Your personal life affects your professional life.
- Start to improve your personal life immediately.

Get Comfortable
With Being Uncomfortable

It's human nature to want to be comfortable. In fact, psychologists tell us that one of the most powerful drives we have is toward comfort. The problem is, this can very often lead to complacency. Once we achieve an acceptable level of comfort, we tend to say (at least we say this on a subconscious level) "Okay, things are fine. I'm comfortable right here. Let's maintain the status quo here now. Let's not rock the boat. Let's not move ahead because that means leaving my comfort zone."

Comfort can be dangerous because it tends to lead to complacency, and complacency is dangerous because it often leads to stagnation. When we do the same old things over and over again, in the same old ways, our minds become dormant, idle, *stagnant*. So do our lives. It's a dangerous state to be in.

In my opinion, *the number one enemy of human progress is complacency* – not problems, not obstacles, not the lack of will or ambition. Complacency.

We mustn't let anything stop our progress. We mustn't sell our future for the trifling price of comfort today.

That's easier said than done, of course. To escape the bonds of comfort, we have to step outside our comfort zones. That takes courage. If we need motivation to do this, we should repeat this phrase to ourselves several times a day: *If I keep doing what I'm doing, I'll keep getting what I'm getting.* For most people, that's a frightening enough thought to be a real motivator.

The Bill Murray comedy movie, *Groundhog Day*, taught an important lesson. Bill's character was literally stuck in the same rut every single day, day after day, until he decided to begin positively changing his thoughts, actions, and attitudes from the inside out. He was comfortable, but he couldn't move on until he stepped out of his comfort zone and changed.

In life, change is constant. We must get used to the "discomfort" of change. Most people like to know what is going to happen in their lives. That's an impossibility. Each and every day is different. We should get used to that fact, and realize that it is okay and natural.

Faith is another essential ingredient in this process of venturing beyond familiar comforts and stepping out into the unchartered territory of change and progress. It's like driving into a tunnel that curves off in another direction. As we drive in, our headlights illuminate only the first part of the tunnel. Beyond the bend, it's completely dark. We have to have belief, going in, that the tunnel does in fact continue on into the darkness beyond the bend ahead and out the other side. And we have to believe that as we approach the dark area, our headlights will light the way before us. It's a question of taking a leap of faith into the darkness because we believe that the outcome will be good.

That's exactly the kind of faith we must have to leave our comfort zones and move ahead. In order to change – to progress – we need to believe and have faith that we'll "come out on the other side of the tunnel."

Then we must *act*. All the faith and belief in the world won't change our lives if we don't actually step outside our comfort zones and start *doing* things differently.

There are a number of practical, everyday exercises that will help us break free from our comfort "chains." They will help us get used to the "extraordinary" and move closer to becoming our personal and professional best. Many of these activities will feel uncomfortable at first, but that's natural. In fact, that's why we ought to do them. Most comforts and discomforts are just our personal interpretations and perspectives about things. They're subjective and emotional. We can change these perspectives – especially when we realize we're growing, learning, and will probably be earning more money because of it.

Here are some of my "get-out-of-your-comfort-zone" favorites ...

Go out and strike up a conversation with someone in a grocery store line, on an elevator, or out on the street.

If we're like most people, we're going to feel a little uncomfortable initiating a conversation with a total stranger. Great! That's the reason why we should do it. Let's upset our poised equilibrium and take a chance! If we want to be successful, we need to be able to be comfortable in dealing and communicating with many different people, all the time. By practicing our own techniques, we'll eventually be able to talk to anyone at anytime, about anything.

As Gene Autry said, "The only strangers I know are simply friends I haven't had the pleasure of meeting yet!"

It may seem almost impossible to do now, but that's natural. It will change in time if we consciously work at it.

Walk up and down your neighborhood and knock on each and every door. Introduce yourself and tell the people you meet who you are and where you live.

I gave one of my clients an assignment to go out and introduce himself to all the neighbors on his street. I did this because he was afraid to speak in public.

I told him to tell them that his teacher told him to do it. I assured him that he'd feel much better and more confident after a few houses. He was amazed how he felt after the exercise. He felt sure of himself. When no one bit him or kicked him, he realized that people are just people, and when approached properly, most of them respond well.

Why not try this ourselves? Isn't it funny that we live our lives so close to others, yet rarely take the time or effort to be more than just strangers to each other? We should take steps to change this, today. It's never too late – even if we've lived and worked around the same people for years. We may even meet people we like and become good friends. It's a great idea to take along a Danish, a pie, or make some friendly gesture. This can serve as an exercise of service and goodwill, as well as a chance to enhance our "people" and social skills. We can be a positive example for our neighbors, and we never know when we might need their help or friendship.

This will help us get outside ourselves. If we do it, we'll feel good afterwards, and proud of our accomplishments.

Dress differently. Change your hairstyle. If you wear glasses, change the style, or get contacts.

The key is for us to look different in some way, which will make us feel different. Remember, we want to look and feel like the progressive new people we are – not the old people who were trapped in their comfort zones.

Two people come to mind. One was a school janitor and the other was temporarily unemployed. They both had low self-esteem. They didn't view themselves as successful and were ashamed and embarrassed about their financial situations. I suggested that they change their appearance.

One gentleman had a mustache, and I suggested that he shave it off. I suggested to the other man that he change his style of glasses and also the way he dressed.

They both followed my advice and instantly felt revitalized. They looked at themselves in the mirror and saw different people. These changes made an immediate difference in their countenances. You could tell they felt better about themselves.

It works!

Changing our appearance is one of the best ways in the world to jump out of our comfort zones. Sure, it's only an outward change, but outer changes stimulate inner changes, and vice versa.

In the cases of these two people, they wanted to earn more money, but couldn't envision themselves as being successful earners. They had never been there before. I knew that they needed to change something about themselves, so they could think of themselves as "new" people – more successful people. When they looked at themselves in the mirror, they no longer saw men who only made $25,000 – they saw men who could achieve much more.

Drive to work a different way. Walk, take a bus, or ride a bike.

We can get into a rut of going to work the same way every day. It can get to the point where we sometimes forget that we're even driving. We climb into our cars, lapse into a comatose-like state, and only wake up when we turn off the ignition.

Wait! We need to break out of our ruts and do something different. How about taking a new way to work? We'll experience new surroundings. We'll feel different. And we'll have to stay awake because we won't be used to the roads. We'll be more aware.

Another alternative is to ride a bike to work or to the store. Whenever possible, I ride my bike to pick up a newspaper, or to rent a video. Instead of driving, I walk to places that are within walking distance. We should change our patterns constantly and keep our conscious minds alert, active, creative, and open to new stimuli.

Do something different during lunch, or during a break in your day.

If we normally go out for lunch, maybe we should stay at work and bring a sack lunch. If we normally eat in at our office, perhaps we should go out. What about taking a walk, meditating, or getting some exercise? How about reading a book or listening to tapes during lunch or breaks?

We should do this more than just once, and change our routines often.

Change your sleep habits.

We should go to bed earlier and get up earlier.

It's amazing what a difference starting and ending the day differently makes. It "kick starts" us into a new mode instantly.

Getting enough sleep makes a real difference, too. This is critical to successful living. It's a source of mental well-being, agility, and energy! It is estimated that over 80 percent of all Americans go without the proper amount of sleep on a regular basis. This is counterproductive to goal attainment.

Eat different foods.

I used to go to the same restaurants and order the same food each time, knowing it was safe – a "sure thing." I knew what it would taste like. I knew I wouldn't be dissatisfied. But I also knew I wouldn't be pleasantly surprised either.

We should go to different places to eat when we dine out, try new dishes, expand our taste, and take "risks."

It's important that we broaden our horizons and force change. The effects will reach far beyond our taste buds. This exercise helps break old habits and patterns which, in turn, will open our minds and unlock our creativity, our thinking, and our potential.

Give volunteer talks at local groups, schools, scout troops, or any organization that is available.

Did you know that public speaking is the number one fear of people in the United States? What a great opportunity to jump out of our comfort zones!

If we have something interesting or informative to say (and if we don't, we can come up with something) we'll find that there are many places and opportunities to speak in public. It's an excellent way to meet people, build confidence, and practice communication skills.

Remember:
- Break out of your comfort zone.
- Change is good.

Just Ask!

There's a lot of money out there that's yours for the taking, or I should say, for the *asking*.

I'm talking about "free" discounts. You'll be surprised how many discounts you can get from many sources – and all you need to do is ask.

When I travel and stay in hotels, I always ask for discounts. Many times the clerk says that they do not "normally" give discounts. I simply treat that response as a mandatory statement which their boss requires them to say. To find out if there's a possibility of a discount, I go further and say "I can appreciate that. However, is there *any* way I can get a discount on my room? It's late and I'll be leaving early in the morning."

It's amazing how often we can get discounts just for asking nicely and being humble and asking for people's help. Everyone likes to help others, and we should give them a chance to help us. And we need to remember that when we ask for something, especially a discount, we should *smile!*

At lumber and hardware stores, I ask for 10 or 15 percent discounts. In the past, when I move, I go to a hardware store and explain to the manager (it's important to ask the right person) that I just moved and want to use his store for all my purchases and would appreciate a discount.

One suggestion: we should make sure that no other customers are around to hear us ask these types of questions. Otherwise, the manager might feel like he has to say no. He is going to want to make it seem like he is doing something special just for us and will not want all the other customers who don't ask for it to hear that he is giving it to us.

Asking for discounts will naturally help us feel comfortable asking for orders, jobs, contracts, and so on. No matter what type of business or profession we're engaged in, we're all in sales, and asking "for the order" is an art that takes practice to master. So we ought to practice by asking for discounts at stores, restaurants, hotels, or wherever we pay for services or goods.

Remember:
*   Ask your way to success.

The "Self-Employed Employee"

It seems funny to me that people make a big distinction between individuals who work for themselves and those who are employees working for a company.

The fact is, we all work for ourselves, whether we're self-employed or employees. When we do corporate trainings, we stress to the employees that in reality they are working for themselves within the structure of a larger company.

If you're an employee, think of yourself as a private contractor with your own one-man company, which has been hired by another company to help it achieve its objectives and become more profitable.

When you view your relationship with your employer in that light, it will make a difference. You will be more motivated to constantly strive to improve your value to your boss and company. You will want to increase your value by learning more, by taking on more responsibilities, by educating yourself in other aspects of the company, by making suggestions, and by helping to do things that are not normally considered to be part of your job.

If you have the attitude that you were hired for one purpose and that is all you have to concern yourself with, and that your day is over when that function is completed, it's time to change your attitude.

Take a more expansive perspective. Think of ways to do what you do better. Think of how your department could function more efficiently. Think of how the company could become more profitable. By opening your mind to these aspects of business, you will stop thinking at the micro level and expand to the macro level.

That is the mark of the kind of person that achieves real

success in a company environment. When you begin thinking at that level, people in high places in your company will notice you and will become aware of your value.

Remember, an employee's security and future potential with a company is only as strong as his value to that company. By increasing your value, you are increasing your job security, and the potential rewards your work will bring you. So never think of yourself as a mere employee. Consider yourself a "self-employed employee" and see the difference it makes.

Remember:
• 	 You are your own employer.

The Mirror Test

I founded a non-profit company called the Inside Corporation. One of its functions and goals is prison reform. I started this program because I don't believe that the government can really rehabilitate prisoners in overcrowded prisons where the libraries don't have a single book by Norman Vincent Peale or Zig Ziglar. To make matters worse, inmates don't trust the "system." Therefore, the private sector must step in and teach them new perspectives and behavior modification. That's what the Inside Corporation is all about.

When I go into state and federal prisons and juvenile detention centers coast-to-coast and speak to inmates, I ask them to take the "mirror test."

You don't have to be an inmate to benefit from the mirror test. In fact, we ask everyone to take the test. It's a fast, direct way to determine where we are today compared to where we want to be. It's quite possibly the most simple yet powerful single exercise I know.

I'd like you to take the mirror test right now.

Grab a piece of paper and a pen. Now find a mirror. Full-length is best, but a bathroom mirror will also work. Make sure no one else is around – just you and yourself.

Now look at yourself in the mirror *directly in the eye*, and speak to yourself out loud. It doesn't matter what you say. Just listen to your voice. This is important.

Look into your eyes. Deeply.

Evaluate what you see. Are you happy? Are you doing the best you can do? Are you sincerely trying to do your best in all aspects of your life?

Now ask yourself Question #1: "What is it that I am doing that I should *not* be doing?"

Write down everything you can possibly think of that

comes to your mind in answer to that question. Don't use anyone's criteria but your own. Don't use your spouse's. Don't use your religion's. Don't use your family's. Go with how *you* feel inside.

Don't rush yourself. Take time to think and reflect. Be completely honest. Remember, this is for you ... there's no sense lying to yourself. After all, you can see right through yourself.

Some of the things you should not be doing may be obvious – smoking, drinking, overeating, and those sorts of things. But there are many that may not be so obvious, such as being sarcastic, swearing, driving too fast, being unkind, and so on. Write down your answers to this important question.

When you're finished with Question #1, it's time to tackle Question #2: "What is it that I am *not* doing that I *should be* doing?"

Again, write down everything that comes to mind – those things that are obvious and those that are not so obvious. Take your time and be honest.

Now that you've listed your responses to both questions, use these answers to set some goals. Make some changes and start to live your life differently.

If you do this, I promise you will feel better about yourself and success will gravitate towards you. Success is predicated to a large extent upon feeling good about ourselves. The better we feel, the more confidence we'll have in ourselves, and the more confidence others will have in us. The more confidence they have in us, the greater our likelihood of success in any endeavor.

Remember:
•   Take the Mirror Test today and often.

Giving and Receiving Compliments

Compliments are powerful!

Let's start today to make a habit of giving people compliments. It's amazing what a positive experience this can be. A compliment can "disarm" people in a positive way, and break down the common barriers that exist between them. It can bring complete strangers closer together in a matter of a few seconds. It can make someone's day.

When we give compliments, people not only feel good about themselves, they feel good about us. They feel accepted, appreciated, and comfortable around us because our positive statements help them feel better about themselves. So the good we do comes back to us.

We'll experience another very significant benefit from giving compliments: we'll begin to look for and see the good in people rather than the bad.

This makes us winners because our perceptions mold our reality, and by seeing people in a more positive light, the world actually becomes a better place for us to live. It also makes the people around us winners because they will try to live up to and even build upon the compliments we pay them. It's no secret that the way we feel about people actually influences how they act.

All our compliments should be sincere, however. Sincere compliments have positive power and energy, while insincere compliments come off as "kissing up."

At first it may be difficult to recognize traits in people worthy of sincere compliments. We need to work at it and find *something*. It will come. There's an old joke about a boy who walks up to an overweight girl in his class, and wanting to say something nice but not seeing much to base a compliment on, says, "Boy, for a fat girl, you sure don't smell too bad!"

Hopefully we'll be able to execute our compliments with more grace, but the idea is valid: we should find *something* good in the people around us – even if it's something relatively insignificant – and use that something as the basis for a sincere compliment.

William Makepeace Thackeray said, "Never lose a chance of saying a kind word. An acorn costs nothing, but it may sprout into a prodigious bit of timber." I think that's great advice.

The flip side of the coin is to know how to receive compliments gracefully. What happens when people give us compliments? What do we say? How do we feel? Do we accept the compliments graciously and thank whoever gave them to us? Or do we try to negate what was said? For example, if someone tells us that we look great, there's a natural tendency to say something like, "Oh come on! I really look horrible!"

If we deny compliments in that way, is it because we're insecure? Are we looking for even more reassurance and reinforcement?

Why not simply acknowledge the compliment with a polite, two-word response to show our appreciation and make the person giving the compliment feel appropriate?

We should simply say "Thank you." If we don't accept compliments graciously with a polite "Thank you," we either feel too good about ourselves or not good enough. Think about it.

I taught my children this at an early age. They are beautiful, and I told them that all of their lives people would say nice things to them about how they look. I taught them that they would never have to feel awkward if they would just smile and say those two magic words, "Thank you."

Let's get in the habit of giving compliments and receiving them graciously. It works.

Remember:
- Accept compliments graciously.

- Give a sincere compliment today and every day for the rest of your life.

The Clutter Monster

Most people laugh when asked about how organized or disorganized their home, desk, office, car, garage, or attic is. They act as if it's funny that it looks like a bomb went off in it.

This is really just a cover-up for the embarrassing reality. The fact is, clutter is not funny – it's a serious matter.

People who live amid clutter generally have no idea of the severely negative impact this has on their minds. Clutter, excess, and disorganization create chaos. They are distracting. They trigger mental frustration and have a negative impact on the subconscious mind.

Most people make attempts to consciously overlook the clutter that surrounds them. Subconsciously though, it can't be ignored. Our conscious mind can be trained to overlook clutter, but our subconscious mind always "sees" it and is deeply affected by it. It's distracting and unnerving to try to function creatively and efficiently around clutter and disorganization. It's like being in a crowded elevator. We want to get out and feel free again. Clutter can actually control us. Our mental state suffers, and that adversely affects our creativity, which in turn affects our success, wealth, and happiness.

On the other hand, a clean, tidy atmosphere frees the mind to explore and be creative. Think about being in a clean, crisp room where everything is in order. This type of environment gives us a feeling of peace, calm, and serenity, which enhances our creativity, our sense of clarity, and our ability to focus.

It's a simple truth: we can clear out our minds by cleaning up around us! Let's fight back and clean up our worlds!

Remember:
- Clean up everything around you *now*!

TV Madness

One of the greatest (and worst) inventions of this century is the television. It's great because it can put us in immediate touch with the world. The coverage of the Persian Gulf War was a prime example of how television can give us instant access to events anywhere in the world.

But television is also an addictive force that can rob us of the motivation we need to fulfill ourselves. Much of what is broadcast on television today is junk. Still, people use TV as an escape or a mental "babysitter." They sit and stare at it for hours. It's an enormous time waster and a distraction from goals.

I challenge you to watch a maximum of only two hours of television per week. If you're addicted like millions of other Americans, then sell, get rid of, or put your TV away for awhile.

Like the alcoholic who thinks he can stop whenever he wants to, we may think we can regulate our use of the television. But we might find that the only way we're going to kick the TV habit is to put it out of our reach and go "cold turkey."

Many people say their reason for watching TV is to "relax" and unwind. Come on! How long does it really take to unwind? We all need to evaluate our personal use of the TV. Does it give us an excuse to avoid more meaningful activities? Do we use it to fill our time so that we don't have to do anything else that requires effort?

Let's all take a good hard look at the time we spend in front of the TV – then "get real" and turn it off. A friend of mine heard a talk at his church when he was 16 years old by a man who advocated turning the television off and using the time to do something constructive. My friend decided he would try it. He went home after the services, and instead of spending the rest of the day watching "the tube" as he usually did, he picked up a book of Rudyard Kipling's short stories and began reading. He spent hours that day with the book, completely absorbed, and was so affected by the great stories he read that he vowed to quit watching television altogether.

He kept his vow all through his junior year of high school. And his senior year. And his college years. In fact, he didn't turn on the television *once* from the time he heard that pivotal talk in church until after he was married *ten years later*. Instead of filling those years with tens of thousands of hours of inane, unmemorable, creativity-destroying television, he read many of the world's greatest books and began writing. Today, he's a successful writer, and he attributes it largely to turning off the television.

If someone watches an average of four hours of television a day and a little more on weekends (and that's below the national average), he'll spend about *15,000 hours* in front of the "boob tube" in the next ten years.

Do you realize what we could do with 15,000 hours in the coming decade? We could build wonderful relationships with our children, our spouses, and our neighbors. We could give loving service to the sick and the needy. We could write novels, movie scripts, plays. We could learn to play several instruments. We could become fluent in several languages. We could earn a doctorate degree – maybe a few. We could become masters in martial arts. We could earn an extra $225,000 at an enjoyable home or hobby business that brings us an average of $15 per hour. (The next time we buy a television, which should last about ten years, add about $225,000 to the sales price and decide whether it's really a good buy after all.)

The point is clear. Let's turn off the television and start really living!

Remember:
- Cut your TV time in half.
- Substitute one hour of activity for one hour of television each day.

Goal-Setting

We've heard it time and time again: "It's critical to set and work toward goals."

Guess what? *It's absolutely true!* We all have dreams, and goal-setting is the key to transforming those dreams into tangible realities.

With goals we can lay out the blueprints and plans for our lives. We can take advantage of one of the great keys to progress: to have something we're working toward at all times. This gives our lives purpose, keeps us moving forward, and promotes personal achievement.

Most people never spend any conscious time thinking about goals and what they really want because subconsciously they feel it will never happen. Well, it certainly won't if they never take the first basic steps to make it happen. This is what goal-setting is all about.

There are a few simple steps we can take to make goals a powerful part of our lives. First, we must make a written list of everything we *want*. It feels very good to do this. It's fun. It will help to clear our minds and crystallize our thoughts.

Next, we need to break down our "wants" into a priority list. We should put them into categories A, B, or C ... depending on their level of importance to us. The attainment of each of these wants is a separate goal.

Now, we establish an action plan for attaining each goal we've set. An action plan is nothing more than a list of steps we must take to turn our wants into realities. We create an action plan by identifying short-range, medium-range, and long-range steps, or objectives, for each goal.

We should determine how long each step will take, and develop a timeline with deadlines for achieving each of the steps toward our goals.

The next step is to develop a list of all possible obstacles that may get in our way. With these in mind, we should decide whose help we can enlist to help us get through them.

Let's not forget to keep track of our progress! I've seen a lot of people work through all of these goal-setting steps, produce a nice, organized notebook of goals, and then get so busy and involved in their daily lives that they never go back to view and review their notes!

We must regularly review our goals and assess where we are in relation to each. It's important to do this daily, or at least weekly. And when appropriate, our goals should be updated. This process of reviewing, accessing, and updating is as important to our success in attaining our goals as our goal-setting process was in the first place!

By following these steps with will and faith, we won't just have to settle for what life dictates or throws our way. We'll make life work for us. I know we'll be a lot happier and more focused, too, because we'll begin to see a clear purpose for our work and activities.

Let's all make a commitment to ourselves *today* and decide to "ride" life just as an equestrian rides a horse. We do this by setting and achieving goals on an ongoing basis. Otherwise, life gets turned around and it "rides" us!

No matter who we are, if we ever hope to rise to great heights, we have to want it, plan for it, write it down, visualize it, and put our plans into action. Let's stop wandering in the dark, and develop a "business plan" for our lives today!

Remember:
- Write down what you want.
- Prioritize.
- Set an action plan.
- Define obstacles.
- Track progress.

Success Prizes

It is vitally important to make life fun and motivate ourselves to greater heights by giving ourselves rewards for the progress we make along the way – for the little successes on our journey to our goals.

For example, if we're trying to lose weight, we should say to ourselves, "If I hit a certain goal weight by a predetermined date, I'll buy a new suit." I know that works for me!

Knowing that we will not only reap the natural rewards of achieving our goals, but will also receive bonuses or prizes when we get there, makes the journey even more enjoyable.

Let's say our goal is to increase our incomes by a certain amount. When we achieve it, we'll have more money, so why not promise ourselves that we'll take a little of it and take a "dream" vacation, or buy something a little extravagant that we've always wanted. As we reach our goals, we have the reason we need to splurge a little and feel good about it.

Perhaps the most powerful benefit of creating a quantifiable reward system that contains incremental compensations is this: our subconscious minds go to work to make our goals realities when meaningful rewards are at stake. This happens automatically. In fact, we couldn't stop it if we wanted to.

So let's set up rewards in advance, and enlist the awesome power of our subconscious minds. If we try it, I'm sure we'll be surprised how well it works.

Remember:
• Celebrate successes with little rewards.

Dream On!

There's one thing we should never overlook, no matter how busy we are: *dreaming*.

We must take time to dream.

This is as important to our physical health as it is to our mental stability. It's relaxing, rejuvenating, and inspiring.

The more we dream, the more we free our subconscious minds to work on our behalf – to direct our lives and create solutions to challenges. After all, inspiration is often no more than a subconscious mind given a goal and left to its own devices. The process of dreaming firmly plants our goals in the soil of our being, and supplies the sunshine and water needed to get them growing.

We need to go to parks or lakes; go for walks through the woods; sit by streams; find quiet spots and time to think. We must turn off the radio or television and take time out for silence.

When was the last time we took a break from our lives, stepped out of our regular routines for a period of time, and really dreamt about what we want our lives to be like? When was the last time we thought about where we would like to be five or ten years from now ... or even next year?

It's vital that we slow ourselves down from time to time. We have to get out of our regular daily environment (it's called "the grind" for good reason) and take time to think about what we really want out of life.

When was the last time we really stopped to think – not to react to something that happened – but to really think about nothing in particular and everything in general?

Remember what I said about organizing ourselves? Let's schedule appointments with ourselves, if that's what it takes, to get away (at least mentally) and take the time to dream.

If by any chance anyone has forgotten how to dream, let me offer a few ideas. One of my favorite "dream exercises" is to think about what it would be like to suddenly be given $10,000 with the stipulation that I have to spend it all on myself. I love to do this. It's like a free vacation. It helps us to learn about ourselves, what we like, and what is most important to us. The outcome of this exercise will be different at different times in our lives.

Another excellent dream exercise is to visualize where we would be and what we would be doing right then if we could be anywhere doing anything. We mustn't limit ourselves. We should let our minds run wild.

Dream! Our dreams will form the foundation and set the course for a successful future.

Remember:
•   Set a dream appointment.

Speak to Me

The single activity people fear the most is public speaking.

Do *you* fear it? What happens when you speak in front of a group of people? Do your palms get sweaty? Do your knees shake? Do you have difficulty regulating your breath?

If you're afraid of speaking in public, have you stopped to analyze why? Is it the fear of rejection? The fear of ridicule? The feeling of inadequacy or insecurity? Don't worry – no matter what your reasons are for fearing it, you're not alone.

The important thing to understand is that anyone *can* overcome that fear. Start by saying: "I want to be a better speaker. I will become a better speaker." Keep saying that until you believe it. Once you do, the rest will be simple.

Here's an exercise. Stand in front of a mirror. Grab a short book or article and read several paragraphs aloud. Read it again and look up into the mirror as much as possible. Maintain eye contact with yourself. Do that every day with a different book or article.

What will this do? First, it will help you become comfortable reading aloud. Most people are very uncomfortable because they don't ever do it. Second, it will help you develop your stage presence by learning how to glance quickly down at your notes for your next thought while maintaining eye contact with your audience (in this case, yourself).

Here's another good exercise. Each day speak to a few people you don't know. This will help you get used to talking with anyone, anytime. The more you do this, the faster your fear will fade away and eventually evaporate altogether.

Next, try preparing and presenting a short speech. Practice it first in front of a mirror. Then present it in front of a video camera. Study the video and take notes on what you seem to be doing right and what you think you need to improve on. Then, following your notes, fix what's wrong and make what's right even better.

Repeat this process as many times as needed. It may take hours, days, even weeks until you feel good and confident about your presentation.

The next step is to deliver your speech to a friend or loved one – someone who will be supportive and positive.

When you've mastered speaking in front of a friend, take the next step up and speak to a small local group or organization. Volunteer to speak at church, a Boy Scout pack meeting, school, or a club to which you belong.

But remember: keep practicing regularly. The mirror and the video camera exercises are great ways to keep your tools sharp and make them even sharper.

Dealing with and speaking to new people is something you'll always have to do in life, so why not get used to it and be good at it? Effective verbal communication is vital to success. The more comfortable you are with it, the easier it will be to get ahead, and the more successful you will be in whatever business you choose.

Remember:
• Get in front of an audience.
• Practice every day with the people you meet.

Typing and Computer Skills

Years ago, executives had immediate access to secretaries who would type their correspondence, reports, and other types of communications. Back then, not knowing how to type was almost a status symbol. It said, "*I'm* too important to do secretarial work. I have someone who does that for me."

Then came the personal computer, coupled with a shift in the American workplace away from huge corporate settings and into smaller offices and home offices.

Suddenly, everyone either wanted to know how to type because they needed to do so to use their computers, or they needed to know how to type because they found themselves without a secretary close by.

The ability to type is no longer an option if we want to be successful. We are in the age of communication. We hold ourselves back if we don't know how to use a computer keyboard efficiently. Typing is a skill we'll use for the rest of our lives. It's necessary in all types of business and in personal life as well. Even many elementary school kids are now using computers to type their reports and homework assignments.

I now know that computer skills are a must. But at first I didn't want to believe it. I tried for a long time to stay as far away from computers as possible. My reason was laziness and the fear of change. I didn't want to dedicate the time and effort necessary to learn the complexities of using a computer. I didn't want to start out as a beginner. No one likes to feel like a child on the first day of school all over again. I wanted to know it all instantly.

Then, when I learned for myself how powerful computers are, and how they could help me become more successful, I knew I had to take time to learn how to use them. I realized that there was really no choice, and no short cut. We are living in an automated society.

I learned on a Macintosh. You can learn how to use one in a matter of a few hours. I can testify to it. The Mac is simple, and easy to use and understand. (With Windows, IBM-compatible computers are also easy to use.) Now I love using a computer. I use it for all my articles, books, and publications. Today I can't imagine how I'd survive without one!

Remember:
- Learn how to type.
- Learn how to use a computer.

Budgets and Savings

One of the most important "power moves" we can ever make is to put our financial lives in order and get the most benefit out of the dollars available to us. Budgeting is one important way we can do this.

Let me tell you about two friends of mine: Peter and Steve. They lived in the same neighborhood in New York. Peter's income was significantly less than Steve's. But Peter had nice furniture, three children in college, two cars, and went on vacations regularly. Steve, on the other hand, drove a "junker" car, had several rooms in his house with no furniture, and couldn't remember the last time he had gone on a vacation.

What's the difference between these two families? Budgeting.

Budgeting is the key to conserving and controlling your financial resources, to knowing where your money goes and staying in control of it.

Peter was frugal and kept track of everything he earned and spent. Steve lived life as his emotions dictated. They both had the means to live comfortably, but Steve could have maintained a much higher lifestyle than Peter's. However, unlike Peter, Steve was not in the habit of living modestly, conservatively, and within a planned budget.

We should all make goals to master our emotions and take active control of our finances. If we spend everything we earn each month, we're going to have to adopt some new habits in order to get ahead.

Unfortunately, most people who spend all their money quickly believe that they'll have money left over if they earn a higher income. The trouble is, if we have poor spending habits, those habits will plague us, no matter how much money we have. Even if we have millions, we'll still go through it like water and end up with nothing saved or left over unless we change our basic philosophy of spending.

The answer is to start today to implement modest living habits and a firm budget in our lives, regardless of our current financial situations.

Another key to living a sound financial life is to have a solid savings plan. One savings plan that really works is extremely simple. I call it the "10 Percent & 10 Percent Plan." Here's what to do:

As soon as we get our paychecks, we take 10 percent and pay it as a tithe to our church or a good charity. We then *pay ourselves* by taking another 10 percent and putting it aside in a savings account. The next step is the hardest: we must live within the remaining 80 percent of our incomes.

The simplest way to do this in the beginning is to pretend that the 20 percent devoted to savings and tithing never existed, or that it was never ours in the first place. That way we won't feel as if we've "short-changed" ourselves in any way. The more diligently we stick to this practice, the easier it will be to increase our level of savings and decrease the amount of income we spend. Things, belongings, and possessions won't have the same meaning anymore. Our desire for them will decrease, and we'll find that the number of material "necessities" in our lives will likewise decrease.

Having to start all over taught me some wonderful lessons. One was that material things are meaningless. What matters most is the family, along with the peace that comes with security. Saving money in the bank – liquid cash – gives much more satisfaction than any purchase we could ever make. Cash in the bank gives security, and there's no way we're going to have cash in the bank unless we choose to save it, rather than spend it.

The kind of savings account I'm suggesting to put the 10 percent into is not the kind of account that is used to save and spend. We must respect our savings enough to leave it alone. We must avoid the temptation to withdraw money unless we absolutely need it for a genuine crisis.

Let's leave it alone and watch it grow.

Remember:
- Live beneath your means.
- Start a savings account today.

Walking and Chewing Gum

We talked earlier about the power of focusing on a single task and excluding all others while doing so.

But some tasks don't require us to focus our total mental energy. I call these "passive activities." We can save time and become much more productive by lumping certain passive activities together and tackling them simultaneously.

In the computer world this is called "multi-tasking."

The idea of doing more than one thing at the same time isn't new or revolutionary. Back in the "days of radio" people did this all the time. Families did a variety of other things while listening to those early radio shows.

Most people don't give the multi-tasking concept enough attention these days. They should, because it's all about efficiency – one of the best ways to accomplish more in the time we have. Time is truly our most valuable resource. Once a minute passes, we can never get it back. Therefore, we must work to make the best use of it, and multi-tasking is a powerful way to do this.

When we go to the doctor's or dentist's office, we could bring a book we can read or work that can be done in the waiting room.

When we watch television, we could exercise at the same time – doing sit-ups, push-ups, or jumping on a rebounder (a mini-trampoline).

When we eat breakfast, we could read a magazine or the newspaper. When we're driving, we could listen to instructional, educational, or motivational tapes. Surveys show that in a five-year period, most people spend enough time in their cars to earn a college degree.

There are many other practical examples of multi-tasking.

We should think of some more ideas, and find ways to incorporate this valuable technique into our own daily lives. It's amazing how many tasks we can do simultaneously, saving time and money.

Remember, time is something we can't produce any more of. Once it's gone, it's gone! So let's use multi-tasking to do more with the time we have.

Remember:
- Use your precious time wisely by multi-tasking.

Journal Therapy

It's important to keep a journal or a diary of our thoughts, feelings, ideas, and activities. I do. I try to write in my journal regularly, and I can attest to the many benefits it brings.

There's something about the physical act of writing down our feelings and putting them into words that makes our thinking become much more clear, more impartial, and more objective. We'll have realizations as we write, and things will surface that we never consciously thought about or understood before.

A journal will serve as a record that will show us objectively how our attitudes and perspectives change over time.

Having our thoughts captured in a journal also helps us realize that nothing is as bad as it seems to be at the moment that it's happening. Everyone has problems. Someone said we can go up to anyone on the street and say, "Hey, I heard about your problem," and the reaction will invariably be, "Who told you?" By writing down how we feel, we get more in touch with ourselves. A therapist listens; a journal does the same thing for free.

When something happens that seems like a "big deal" or a momentous problem, writing it down helps us blow off steam and release it. When we go back to our journal later, chances are that our problem won't seem so monumental. It's amazing how the things that we are so concerned about today will appear to be little more than insignificant details a year from now. The feeling is similar to looking at old pictures and reminiscing, except that we get the words and the feelings as well. We'll learn a lot about who we are and what our lives are all about just by listening to ourselves as we read our journals.

Another benefit of keeping a journal is reserved for the future, when we look back and see how much we've grown and overcome. Knowing what we were feeling at a specific time in our lives and comparing it to our current situation will reveal many things to us. It will show us how we've progressed, how we've tapped into more of our potential, and how we've climbed to greater heights.

Keeping a journal is not difficult, but it takes commitment. It's important to write in it on a regular basis. We don't have to make entries every day if it feels like a chore. This should be something that we enjoy. If we don't enjoy it, we won't do it for long.

On the other hand, we shouldn't wait for "free time" or some other convenient chance to write. That may never happen, and we'll never get any journal writing done. Instead, we should make a flexible schedule for ourselves – one we can live with. We might set a goal, for example, to write in our journals three times per week, or perhaps every other morning or evening.

We should date all our entries and keep them in a hard-bound or spiral notebook. We can even use a computer. Keeping a journal in a computer has advantages, because we can instantly search for specific dates, names, or key words. It also has disadvantages, because even the small notebook computers aren't as portable and convenient as a paper notebook. If we keep our journal on a computer, it's very important to regularly back up the data, and print hard copies just in case.

We ought to treat our journals like friends – like someone we can talk to openly. We talk to friends because we want to, not because we have to. That's how we should feel about our journals.

One excellent suggestion I heard was to use our journals as mini-scrapbooks, too. That way we can keep our important pictures and memorabilia all in one place. A year, ten years, 50 years from now, we'll experience great joy sitting down and looking back over what was happening in our lives before.

The experience of keeping a journal is one of life's most satisfying and useful activities. Let's not miss it!

Remember:
- Start a journal today.
- Use it as a friend and a therapist.

Back to the Basics

When life gets difficult, or when things start going the opposite way we want them to go, I find that it's good to go back to the basics. Sometimes we get too "fancy" and forget the basic fundamentals.

I'll never forget my grade school basketball coach, Mr. Herman. He would make us do lay-ups for hours and hours. He said he didn't want to see us shooting outside shots when we could be shooting lay-ups, which are more likely to go in the basket. He taught us that the basics – running, dribbling, passing, and lay-ups – would get us farther than the fanciest shots in the world. Of course, we all wanted to shoot those fancy shots to show our prowess on the court, but he said, "No! I want you making lay-ups. Run them into the ground. Don't forget the basics and get fancy." Mr. Herman's teams won several championships using that philosophy.

It's amazing what we can do with just the basics. What wonderful and complex music a master can make on the violin! And yet it has only four strings. Just so, if we master the basic principles of success, we can create a symphony of prosperity and happiness in our lives.

Remember:
- Never forget the basics.

Key 4:

FEELING GREAT ABOUT OURSELVES

Stop! You're Hurting Me!

If we want to be successful, we've got to feel good about ourselves.

Self-esteem is in short supply these days. People everywhere are suffering because they don't feel very good about themselves.   It's extremely difficult to succeed at anything if our self-esteem is low. On the other hand, when we feel good about ourselves, success seems to flow naturally.

There are many reasons for low self-esteem, but there are just as many ways to turn the tide and develop a solid, healthy respect for ourselves. And we can start doing it today.

How? One of the best ways to develop a healthy self-esteem is to kick a negative habit. If we're honest with ourselves, we can think of habits we want to get rid of – habits that perhaps we've even tried to break before, but haven't yet been able to. These habits could be anything from smoking and drinking, to the seemingly insignificant but detrimental things that only *we* know about ourselves.

There's a story about a young man who was made the victim of an unkind practical joke by some friends. They put a heavy stone in his backpack before they started to climb a mountain. The hiker struggled as he carried it up the mountain, and eventually fell to the back of the hiking group. It finally weighed him down so much that he eventually had to stop and let the others go on without him.

The rock, like a bad habit, was a useless burden to carry – a burden that stopped his progress. If we have a bad habit that's weighing us down, we need to take it out of our packs and leave it behind. We should rid ourselves of the useless baggage of negative habits. They keep us from climbing to the peak of our potential.

If we pick out a negative habit in our lives and start working to eliminate it today, our self-esteem will rise this very day, and we'll feel better about ourselves each day that we continue to succeed in conquering that habit.

Our confidence will grow. We will trust ourselves more. And when we finally feel free of that habit, not only will we reap the natural rewards of not participating in that negative behavior anymore, but we'll also have larger "I-can-do-it" muscles because we've exercised them and made them grow. That means it will be even easier to overcome the next negative habit on our lists.

All of this creates positive momentum that will spill over into almost every aspect of our personal and business lives.

I'd like to share a few tips for breaking habits. First, when we make the decision to eliminate a bad habit, we shouldn't say to ourselves that we're going to try to quit, or that we want to quit, or even that we're in the process of quitting. Instead, we should say, "I *have* quit! I don't do that anymore."

I was consulting with a client who was a heavy smoker. He had quit several times before. I asked him if he was going to quit smoking again.

He said, "Yes." I asked, "When?" He said, "Now," and threw his cigarettes in the trash can.

I waited a few minutes and asked him if he smoked. He said "Yes, but I'm *trying* to quit."

I asked him if he was smoking at that moment.   H e looked at me strangely and said "No! You can see I'm not."

I told him if he wasn't smoking *at that moment*, he'd already quit! What he had been doing was projecting his past experiences into the future by saying he was only "trying" to quit. I wanted him to forget the past, think only of the present, realize he wasn't smoking now and wasn't going to in the future because he made this firm decision in his mind.

From that moment on, he stopped smoking completely.

The mind is a powerful tool which we can use to break negative habits and establish positive ones. If we haven't had success breaking habits in the past, we must reprogram our conscious and subconscious minds. It's like wiping a table clean or cleaning off a blackboard. We have to clean the slate and start fresh. We have to forget the past and move on.

Let's give our conscious minds definitive input, and they will work to make it a reality. It's that simple.

I'm not saying it's always easy, however. But once we understand and truly know that *we* are in charge of how and what we think, we've moved much closer to mastering ourselves.

Second tip: let's pretend that every day is New Year's Day. After all, isn't that when we get all fired up to make resolutions? Bad habits shouldn't wait until next January 1st, however. So let's tackle them today. There's nothing that says today can't be as good a day to start as the first day of a new year.

Tip number three: we should make a list of *all* our bad habits right away, but avoid setting ourselves up for failure by attacking them all at once, or even by taking on one of the toughest ones right off the bat. Would we walk into a weight room and try to bench press 300 pounds without building up our muscles first? Of course not. Similarly, we should target the easier habits first and get rid of them, one after another, working our way up to the weightier ones as our willpower muscles become stronger.

Every day that we continue to allow our negative habits to rule us, we move further and further away from our full potential. But each day we do war against even a small negative habit, we're moving closer to our ideal selves.

Remember:
- Throw out bad habits that weigh you down.
- Make a fresh, winning start today.

Minding Our Manners

It's difficult to build or maintain self-esteem if people avoid us or become offended by us because of our manners.

We all should have been taught manners and politeness as children, but unfortunately many of us did not get this training.

I don't mean just opening the door for others. I mean learning manners for table etiquette, social etiquette, verbal communications, and more. Several books have been written on the subject of manners and etiquette. I strongly suggest that we read some of them and learn to become true gentlemen or genteel women.

Being polite and having impeccable manners will help us advance in our professional lives. It paves the way to new relationships. It elevates our status in the eyes of others, and gives us a positive, polished image.

Mishandling situations because of poor manners or etiquette, even in ways we might think are insignificant, has been the cause of many unfortunate personal and business losses. It's much better to properly educate ourselves right now, so we can be prepared for all situations that might arise in the future.

A friend of mine was telling me about a friend of his – a handsome, well-to-do, 47-year-old bachelor who has everything a man could want except good table manners. He somehow missed this phase of his education, and no one has had the courage to point out to him his shortcoming. Although this man has been successful in his career, there have been opportunities he has missed and relationships that haven't developed because his horrible table manners turn people off at business lunches with associates and intimate dinners with dates.

I remember a speaker I knew who hadn't learned that it's

poor etiquette to call attention to the fact that a woman is pregnant unless she brings it up herself. This poor man, in a public setting, asked a woman, "When are you due?" Well, she wasn't pregnant at all – just overweight. A little education in manners would have saved both the woman and the speaker some serious embarrassment.

We need to develop excellent manners and make them a habit in our lives. We'll feel better about ourselves, and others will, too.

Remember:
- Learn etiquette.
- Make your manners work for you – not against you.

The Eyes Have It

Have you ever tried to talk to someone who won't look you in the eye? How did that make you feel? If you're like most people, you felt like the person was either not interested in what you were saying, had low self-esteem, or was not telling the truth about something.

We must avoid the habit of not looking people in the eye. Like poor manners, this habit will take its toll on our self-esteem.

I taught my children at a very young age that when they talk to other people, they must look them in the eyes. They established this habit early in life and it has helped them.

Start now to become aware of your own eye contact when you're with other people. Be conscious of where you are looking every time you speak with someone. Work to develop eye contact that is consistent and strong. Practice and train yourself. You'll be amazed at the positive benefits it will bring.

Eye contact is powerful. Put it to use in achieving your goals.

Remember:
• Utilize the power of eye contact.

Grip It Tight

A firm handshake – like direct eye contact – is essential to making a good impression in our society. A firm, assertive handshake tells people that we have self-esteem and confidence.

A weak handshake, on the other hand (no pun intended), gives the other party the message that we are unsure of ourselves and uncertain about what we are doing.

Even if that message is not true now, it soon will be, because a weak, "fishy" grip will turn others off and influence the way they feel about us, which sooner or later will influence the way we feel about ourselves.

The social ritual of shaking hands is a powerful and important part of our culture – a key factor in the creation of first and ongoing impressions. The handshake has endured through several centuries, and will certainly be around a lot longer than *we* are.

So let's get a grip! When we shake someone's hand, we should grasp it firmly and shake assertively. (We mustn't overdo it, however – there's a difference between firm and painful.) We'll immediately feel stronger and better about ourselves, and so will the people whose hands we're shaking.

Remember:
- Be the first to shake hands, and do it firmly.

The Good Stuff List

One of the best and easiest things we can do to boost our self-esteem is to make a Good Stuff List.

All we have to do is list between 10 and 20 things about ourselves that are good, positive, or favorable. However great or small they may seem to us, these are our assets.

Here is a hypothetical example of a Good Stuff List: "I am a good father. I have a successful marriage. I have a steady income. I work out regularly. I am a good tennis player. I tell jokes well. I go to church regularly. I am a good Little League coach. I have gone more than three years without getting a speeding ticket. I can cook up a mean dish of steamed vegetables. I am a good speller. I like to do nice things for people."

It's important to create this list when we're already feeling good. We should keep the list in a permanent place, like a journal, and update it periodically. And we should refer back to it whenever we're feeling low. It will help raise our spirits, and get us moving in a positive direction again.

Remember:
•   Make a Good Stuff List *now*.

No Sarcasm or Mockery For Me

Another way to improve our self-esteem is to look for the positive in ourselves and others. We can't do that if we've developed the pernicious habits of sarcasm and mockery, which feed on the negative aspects of people.

Let's cut sarcasm and mockery out of our lives!

No one likes them. They are often offensive to others. And they're usually only amusing to the person who is verbalizing them. Plus, these traits are highly contagious and have reached epidemic proportions in our society. Sarcasm and mockery are habits that are easy to develop and difficult to get rid of. Like other negative habits, they tend to get progressively worse as time goes on. So we must cast them out of our lives *now*.

How do you feel about a person whom you hear mocking, ridiculing, or being sarcastic about someone else? If you're like most people, this kind of behavior causes you to think less of the people who indulge in it. It reflects negatively on their personality, morals, and character. It's easy to lose respect for someone like this, and it's difficult to want to open up to them. Why? Because we know that if they mock people behind their backs, they will sooner or later mock us behind ours.

We should commit to this simple rule: "I will never mock, put down, or say anything at the expense of someone else."

Let's open our ears and listen to ourselves. Let's catch ourselves when we say or think something mocking or sarcastic.

If we begin today to cast these habits out of our behavior, we will improve our image in the eyes of other people, and more importantly, in our own.

Remember:
•   Become aware and never engage in sarcasm and mockery.

Looking for the Child Within

A man by the name of Sydney Harris once said, "When you confront a man who shows unattractive traits ... see him as the child he was. Remember that he began his life with laughing expectancy, with trust, with warmth, desiring to give love and to accept love. And then remember that something happened to him... something he is not aware of... to turn the trust into suspicion, the warmth into wariness, the give-and-take into all-take and no-give. See him as the child he was."

This is wonderful advice. But it becomes especially powerful when we apply it to ourselves.

We should look for the child within others and within ourselves. This will not only help us accept others and look to them as individuals and as friends, but will enable us to accept ourselves, forgive ourselves, and to actually like ourselves more. Once that happens, self-improvement and self-esteem will follow.

Remember:
• Every adult is just a grown-up child in a big body.

Key 5:

ADJUSTING OUR PERSPECTIVES

Looking at the Good Side

We're on our way to an important appointment. Suddenly we feel our car pull to the right, then feel the telltale shimmy of a flat tire. We pull over, get out of our car, and sure enough, our tire is completely flat. There's no service station in sight.

How do we feel about what has just happened? How are we going to look at it?

What are our choices? One is to feel total frustration and see the incident as a curse. But that's not the only perspective we could take. We could also feel calm and accepting about it, and see it as a positive experience – even a blessing.

How? It could be that if we would have kept driving, a truck would have gone through a red light at the next intersection and smashed into us, crippling us for life, or maybe killing us. Or perhaps, we'll meet someone who stops to help us on the road, and we'll sell him a big insurance policy or make an important business contact of some type.

We can look at the bright side of anything. We can turn every apparently negative thing that happens to us into something positive. Everything that happens can be viewed positively or negatively, so why shouldn't we choose to see things in a positive light?

How we go about turning negatives into positives isn't as important as getting into the habit of doing it. We should make it second nature, so that it takes place subconsciously and instantly.

It's a question of perspective. I heard a beautiful saying once. It goes, "I had the blues, because I had no shoes, until upon the street, I met a man who had no feet." Sure, we could have it better, but we could always have it worse. If we don't appreciate what we've got, watch out! It could be taken away from us in a minute.

We all have problems. Norman Vincent Peale once said that the only time he found people without problems was when he walked through a cemetery. So let's accept our problems, turn them into opportunities, and think of all the good things in our lives. Let's focus on the positive side rather than the negative.

It's funny – when we ask people how we're doing at work, we'll often hear them groan that they're "swamped." But if they weren't swamped, they'd probably be out of a job, in which case they would be groaning far louder. So they really should look upon being swamped as a blessing – something that is keeping them employed and providing them with job security.

Speaking of employment, what if tomorrow you lost your job? How would you react? If you're like most people, you'd be angry, afraid, and then sink into depression. All this would become a major obstacle in finding a new way to make a living.

That's how most people would react. But remember, you're *not* like most people. The fact that you're reading this book is proof that you're not. So let me suggest a far better way to look at such a situation: think of it as the best thing that's ever happened.

You're probably questioning my sanity at this point. How on earth can I possibly ask you to consider getting fired the best thing that's ever happened to you?

Easy. Thousands of wealthy people will back me up. The world is full of multimillionaires who look back on the day they lost their jobs and say, "Thank heaven I was forced to leave that dead-end job, because if I hadn't, I never would have gotten into what I'm doing now." Lee Iacocca is just one of the people who see that experience as a blessing in disguise.

As we're getting into the habit of looking at the good side of things, let's not forget to look at the good side of *ourselves*. We will do better, go farther, and be happier if we focus on our strengths rather than our weaknesses. We all know that forgiveness is important. Let's learn to forgive ourselves, and then move ahead in our journey of self-improvement. It helps to surround ourselves with positive people and positive stories about people, like those found in *Success* and *Entrepreneur* magazines, which feature inspiring stories about real people like us.

Remember:
- Always see the positive!
- See only the good.

Counting Our Blessings

I'd like to share with you a simple but powerful trick for improving our perspectives.

Many people who have read my autobiography have told me they never would have been able to make it through the difficult challenges I experienced. They wanted to know how I was able to control my thoughts and actions and keep going.

I did it by forcing a change in my perspective. I compared myself to others who had been in much more difficult situations. This changed my perspective for the better immediately. It made me stop lamenting how tough I had it, and instead focus on how fortunate I really was to be dealing with my situation, instead of facing something much worse.

Victor Frankl wrote a wonderful book called *Man's Search For Meaning,* about his personal experience as a prisoner of the Nazi concentration camps in World War II. It's an inspirational book that we should all read. I found it to be much like the story of Job in the Bible – except that it happened in our day and age.

When we think about what so many other people have had to go through in life, we won't be able to feel sorry for ourselves any more. Instead, we'll want to count our many blessings.

We must realize that whatever we're dealing with, it could be much worse. We should realize this now and make a conscious decision to adopt a more positive attitude and perspective about our situations. Let's be happy and work to feel and believe it with all our strength. Others who have gone before us have set inspirational examples for overcoming adversity. We can, too!

Remember:
- Be grateful for who you are and what you have.
- If you are alive today, you are a success!

We're in Complete Control

There are many aspects of our lives that we can't control. A car could run a red light and cripple us for life. Someone could sneeze in the elevator and give us a cold. The controller of the company we work for could run away with all the money, forcing the business into bankruptcy and sending us out to look for work.

But we *are* in control of the most important aspect of our lives: how we view and react to what's happening to us. We are in full control of our own perspectives.

Unfortunately, most people turn over that control to others. They let others dictate how they view and react to life.

Let's make the conscious decision to *act* rather than react to the events of our lives. Our minds can exert influence over our emotions to control our perspectives. No one can *make* us feel anything. The emotions we feel and our perspectives are chosen by us and no one else.

Someone can slap us in the face, but no one can make us react by striking back or running away in anger and humiliation. Whether we realize it or not, only *we* can allow a particular feeling to exist inside us. We make that decision ourselves.

What if someone slapped us and we refused to react violently or become angry? What if someone zipped into the parking stall we'd been waiting for and we refused to let it bother us? What if our bosses or one of our major customers attacked us verbally for no apparent reason and we quietly listened without letting it get to us? What if we took complete control of our perspectives and all our reactions, and decided not to let any event affect our days negatively?

Imagine the power we would have! It is an incredibly awesome power. A complete power. And it is one of the most important powers we can have, because what happens *to* us is not nearly as important as *what we do* with what happens to us. If we cultivate this power, it will give us the strength to do virtually anything we really want to do in this world.

Remember:
- Understand that we have ultimate control over ourselves and our perspectives.
- Act. Don't react.

Turning Our Work Into Play

Would you believe me if I told you that by merely changing our perspectives about work, we wouldn't have to work another day of our lives?

It's true.

All we have to do is turn our work into play. Then we can spend the rest of our lives playing!

When I was a boy delivering newspapers, I used to pretend that the mats in front of the houses were catcher's mitts. I would try to throw the papers so that they would land on top of the mat. Those would be "strikes." I was the pitcher of my little league baseball team at the time, so this challenge made my job a game. It was fun for me. You see, I wasn't delivering newspapers – I was throwing strikes.

I turned my work into play.

Even adults can play this game. (After all, we're the ones who really need it!) The first real estate property I ever owned had a driveway that needed to be dug up to make room for the yard. I could have viewed it as a back-breaking, tedious job that I was going to hate. Instead, I decided to change my perspective and see it as a weight-lifting experience. I pretended I was just exercising, and the back-breaking work turned into play!

A few of my friends even came over and got in on the "fun." We'd all get together after work in the evening and dig and shovel until one or two o'clock in the morning. We'd fill up a rented pick-up truck until it was barely movable, then drive it to a place where construction workers were filling in a burned-out building's basement, where we'd shovel the dirt and asphalt into the hole.

The philosopher Friedrich Nietzsche once said, "In man there is hidden a child who wants to play." When we use a positive perspective to turn work into play, we'll find that the child inside us will take over and get the job done in a fun and surprisingly effective way.

Remember:
- Find a way to view your work as play – then play, play, play!

We Don't Know Until We Know

When we have the right perspective about life, we'll naturally assume that every response is a "Yes!" until we're absolutely sure that it's not.

Here's an example. When I was selling siding door-to-door in New York, I was teaching a new recruit which houses to call on. Since we were selling vinyl siding, every house that didn't already have vinyl siding on the exterior was a prospect.

We came to a house that had a huge sign on the door that said "No solicitors. No salespeople of any kind. If you are selling something, do not stop here!" We stopped anyway and spoke to the owners of the house. By the end of the evening, we had sold the couple siding for their home.

Just before leaving, I decided to ask about the sign. The couple started to laugh and explained that they had just moved in and hadn't gotten around to taking down the sign, which the previous owners had left.

Most salespeople would have walked past this house, taking the sign's negative message at face value. But we didn't, and consequently we put a huge commission in our pockets!

Another sales recruit in the same company, named Joel, was out knocking on doors his first week. He went to every house, just as he was told to, because he didn't want to lose his new job. He even went to the houses that already had aluminum siding on them (remember, he was selling vinyl siding). Because he did this, he made several big sales to homes that already had aluminum siding. In most cases, they were new homeowners who were already unhappy with the present siding and wanted a change.

One day, Joel stopped at a house where the owner was in the back yard on a ladder painting the house. He was almost finished with the project. He had burned off all the old paint with a torch. He had sanded the wood, primed it, and then painted it with two coats of high-grade paint.

The home owner had put a lot of work into painting his house that summer, and was nearly finished.

Would *we* have asked this man if he wanted to cover his new paint job with vinyl siding? Not likely.

But Joel did. And guess what? He made a sale! The man bought siding that night because he vowed never again to spend his entire summer painting his house!

Maintain a positive perspective. Always assume that the response will be a "Yes!"

Remember:
• Always expect a "Yes!"

Sharpening Our Axes

There's a story of two men who were in a wood-chopping contest. Both men had equal strength and skill, good axes, and a huge pile of wood before them. With the crack of a gun, the contest began.

One man chopped energetically without stopping. He felt that he would win because the other man, whom he could see over at the other end of the field, kept stopping every 15 minutes to rest. After two hours, the man across the field put down his ax, having chopped all the wood, and was proclaimed victor.

The man who had been chopping without stopping was baffled. He was still about an hour away from finishing. How could the other man have finished so quickly when he had stopped to rest every 15 minutes?

He soon had his answer. The other man hadn't stopped to rest at all. He had stopped every 15 minutes to sharpen his ax!

Let's keep our "axes" of positive perspective sharp. Establishing and maintaining a positive attitude requires daily attention. It can be easily lost. It can quickly get "dull." We must work every day to safeguard our attitudes. We should constantly monitor our speech, our thoughts, and our acts, and keep this most powerful tool sharp. It's critically important to take time out regularly to regroup and refine our actions and thoughts. We must continually sharpen our axes to reach our full potential.

Remember:
* Sharpen your skills and your attitude regularly.

Key 6:

EMBRACING THE CHANGE

Forwards or Backwards?

The only thing that is constant in this life is change. Change is everywhere. It's happening all the time. The ancient Taoist sages said that it's impossible to step in the same river twice, because no matter how quickly we put our feet into the stream the second time, it will not be the same water that flows by it.

We are like rivers. Even when asleep, we're in a constant state of flux. Billions of chemical changes are fired off in our cells every second. Blood flows through us. Our senses are constantly reacting to outside stimulation. We think. We act. We can no more stay the same – even for a nanosecond – than the river.

We may sometimes feel like we're not changing, but we are always moving either forwards or backwards, no matter how hard we fight it. This is as it should be, because all growth and progress are the result of change.

I read a book entitled *Grow or Die*. The title is so true. We're always either progressing or regressing in every aspect of our lives. Day in and day out, everything we think and do tips the scales in one direction or the other. It's as if every thought and every deed, large or small, is a pebble that is dropped onto either the positive tray or the negative tray on the scale.

Once we realize this, we'll start to place much more value on *every single thing* we do. We now see that all we do literally affects us either in a positive or negative way. This is a very important concept to grasp. The sooner we realize this, the sooner we'll be able to eliminate negative and unproductive thoughts and actions. We'll soon see that engaging in those kinds of thoughts and actions will only hold us back from reaching our goals.

Remember:

- Use change as a propellor to move forward.

Cocoons of Change

"How do we become butterflies?"

"We must want to fly so much that we are willing to give up being caterpillars."

Most of us are like caterpillars. Yet within each of us is a beautiful butterfly waiting to be freed! The trouble is, we've become too comfortable as caterpillars, even though they are slow-moving, not very pretty, and accustomed to crawling in the dirt. The fear of change has made us willing to go on crawling in the dirt rather than making the commitment to shed our old selves and soar through the sky – light, free, and beautiful.

When we think of initiating change within ourselves, most of us feel uncomfortable, or even anxious. It's perfectly natural to feel uneasy about change. There's nothing wrong with feeling that way. We all feel it. It's part of being human.

A friend told me that earlier in his life, whenever he felt that a change was imminent, he would stop whatever he was doing or thinking. It was as if a red flag popped up and said, "Potential danger! Discomfort ahead!"

He has since learned to ignore those red flags and push ahead anyway. Successful, achievement-oriented individuals move forward in spite of those feelings because they understand that change is the avenue to personal and professional progress.

We must realize that before we can unlock our full power and potential and *Change!*, we are going to have to make a lot of little changes in our lives on a continuous basis, and that it will often be awkward or difficult. We must be willing to pay that price as our "investment" for the reward of being the best we can possibly be.

Butterflies are not born as butterflies. They go through stages of development and must eventually break free from their own cocoon. We too must work to free ourselves from our own cocoons of comfort and grow into our best selves. Just as the butterfly transforms itself from the awkward, lowly, caterpillar into the magical, soaring creature that it is, we can do the same with our own lives.

When we compare the cost to the reward, the willingness to change is a very small price to pay. Let's learn to enjoy this process of change. After all, it's a lifelong journey.

Remember:
- Don't resist change.
- Soar with it!

Exercises for Change

Change can come in many forms. It can be as simple as taking a pottery class, or as major as moving from Florida to Oregon.

Do we ever feel apprehensive or uncomfortable about going to parties, speaking in public, changing jobs, or talking to new people? Do those feelings ever stop us from doing those things? If so, it's time for an attitude adjustment. We need to change our mental attitude so it can begin to work for us rather than against us.

We should form a new habit with the way we view change. After all, change was, is, and will always be a part of our lives, so it's best for us to find a successful way to deal with it and make it work for us.

The next time apprehension and discomfort rear their ugly heads and threaten to stop us from doing something we know would be good for us, let's recognize those feelings, acknowledge why we have them, and then make them a positive signal to initiate a change. From that point on, whenever such a feeling grips us, we can just say, "Ah! There it is again – the signal that I have another opportunity to face my fears and do something that will help me change and progress."

Readjusting our attitudes in this way will help us overcome those negative feelings and move ahead.

It also takes practice. We've already discussed getting out of our comfort zones and purposefully doing things that make us feel apprehensive and uncomfortable. This is an excellent way to get comfortable with change.

A gentleman I know gave a talk entitled, "Walk across the dance floor." The talk was about doing things we feel uncomfortable doing. The title of his talk referred to junior high school dances in the gym, where the girls are on one side and the guys on the other. He was explaining about how each guy would have to "walk across the dance floor" to ask the girls to dance. The walk over wasn't their only challenge, he pointed out – it was the long walk back if she said "No!" to his request.

We've got to learn to get out of our comfort zones before we can hope to embrace change and get what we want in our lives.

My older sister wanted to go to the senior prom when she was only a sophomore in high school. She was nice-looking, outgoing, and not afraid to step outside her shell. She didn't want to wait around to see if some guy was going to ask her to the dance, so she did the asking.

She must have asked a half dozen guys before she got a yes. But she did get a yes!

She had a goal and she achieved it by doing something that all her friends were afraid to do. She was rewarded for her efforts because instead of sitting home and missing an exciting event, she went to the senior prom as a sophomore and had a wonderful time!

One day I was in the airport waiting to get on a flight when I saw Terry "Hulk" Hogan. I wanted to talk to him because I was impressed with how he had made a name for himself and created an image. I just went up to him and told him exactly that.

He was genuine, kind, and thoughtful. Who would have thought from his tough, brazen public image that he would be so approachable? When I told him I was impressed by what he had done with his career, he said he was just getting started.

Afterwards I felt good about myself and about him, and gained greater confidence to talk to other celebrities in the future. By pushing myself out of my comfort zone, I made a positive change in my life.

One of my clients, James, is another good example. He and two of his partners had come to my office for a consultation. After they left, in the car, James said he wanted to go back and get a picture of himself with me. The other partners felt uncomfortable about the idea, thinking that it would inconvenience me. James said that he knew he *should* do it, because the others felt uncomfortable about it.

They drove back to my office and came in with their camera and got their picture taken with me. I felt honored that they would want to do that and they were all happy that James had insisted on coming back!

I had a similar experience. One evening I was invited to dinner at Georgia Governor Zell Miller's home. I wanted to have a photo of me taken with him and his wife, but I felt a little apprehensive about asking. I asked someone there to take the picture anyway, and now I have that picture as part of my permanent photo collection.

There are many things we can do to snap ourselves out of our comfort zones and get used to change. How about hot air ballooning, skydiving, scuba diving, or traveling somewhere new? We could go to a mall and start a conversation with several retail people in the stores, sit somewhere other than where we normally sit at the dinner table, or wear our watches on our other wrists. Let's do things we've never done before!

These changes will help us feel new and different, and can dramatically alter our thinking and perceptions. They will put us in a new frame of mind, and will propel our minds to a place where they can more easily accept and pursue positive change.

The uneasiness we may feel when we are training ourselves to break out of our comfort zones and become comfortable with change will soon be replaced with a sense of self-satisfaction and accomplishment.

Remember:
- Look at change as an opportunity.
- Do the uncomfortable.

Feel Good About Every Little Step

During the ongoing process of changing from what we were to what we want to become, it's easy to become frustrated with ourselves. This is because as we progress, new vistas of potential open up to us, and we realize how much farther there is to go to get where we want to be. It's just like knowledge: the more we know, the more we realize we don't know.

We mustn't let this frustration knock us off the path. We should just be the best that we can be, and keep moving ahead no matter how slow our progress seems. Many people bring undue stress on themselves by believing they must be perfect, and then striving unsuccessfully to attain that state of perfection. There is simply no way, as humans on earth, to attain complete and total perfection. So let's give ourselves a break and just concentrate on being the best that we can be right now.

It's important to avoid discouragement, and remember that nothing valuable comes overnight and nothing good comes quickly. Maybe we aren't reading a book a day, but at least we're reading a few pages a week. If that's more than we were doing before, then we should pat ourselves on the back for being on the right road. Aren't we running five miles a day yet? Are we just walking around the block a few times? That's better than nothing – and if it's more than we were doing last month, it's progress.

Many "littles" add up to "a lot," and even progress measured in inches eventually adds up to miles.

The key is to move forward little by little, tackling our goals bit by bit. If we take little steps forward every day, we will eventually reach our goals. What's more, just the fact that we're moving in the right direction will help us accelerate our progress, because we'll become stronger and more motivated with each step we take.

Consistency is the key. A great pianist once admitted, "If I don't practice one day, I know it. If I don't practice the next day, the orchestra knows it. If I don't practice the third day, the whole world knows it."

If a prominent, gifted pianist has to practice and use his talents every day, how can we expect to move forward without the same kind of consistency? Just keep "plugging away," and our dreams will come true. But we must do it day after day after day.

Remember:

- Place only realistic expectations on yourself.
- Small, consistent steps are key to progress.

Key 7:

CHARTING THE COURSE

Charting Our Way to Excellence

I want to let you in on a powerful life-improvement system that's based on record-keeping. I refer to it as "charting."

Simply stated, charting makes the path toward our goals more visible and attainable. It's a very effective goal-achievement tool – a great way to physically keep track of our objectives in life and monitor our progress toward them. But even more importantly, by giving us instant and ongoing feedback and continuously illustrating our success, charting actually motivates us, both consciously and subconsciously, to reach our goals.

Our successes may seem insignificant from one day to the next, but when we record our progress on charts, we can see our overall improvement over a period of time. This helps us build momentum and maintain our enthusiasm. Achieving small successes continuously and being able to see on charts how those little accomplishments add up to significant advancements is crucial to our success. This is what the chart system can do for us.

Let's face it, how long will we remain excited about our goals if we go out and are beaten down each day without a long-term perspective?

The chart system can provide a means of maintaining a long-term perspective, and can be used in all aspects of our business and personal lives. It is a unique goal-fulfillment tool that can be applied to any area of life where desires and objectives have been established.

This system of charting has worked for me and many others without fail. If done right, it's a "sure thing." When I say "do it right," I mean that we must be diligent in doing what the charts demand, and we must stay current and active with our charting. But even if we don't do it right – even if we occasionally slip – the simple act of charting will in itself increase our probability and level of success.

The chart system is extremely versatile. I've used it in many different ways to help me get what I truly wanted out of life. You can, too. Charts can help us rise to higher levels of achievement in virtually any facet of our business or personal lives. Whether we want to make more sales per month, lose weight, or develop a closer relationship with our children, charting can help us do it.   Another aspect of the versatility of charts is that they're flexible. They can be designed to track a single objective or many objectives on the same chart simultaneously.

Charts can also be set up to track our progress at any time interval we choose. Most charts are daily, but some are weekly. Others may be monthly or quarterly. Some may even be hourly on the short end of the time spectrum, or yearly on the long end. For example, a chart to help us make a minimum number of sales calls per day would probably be a daily chart. But not necessarily. We might find it helpful to break the day down into before-lunch and after-lunch periods, or into hourly intervals, and set a goal to make a certain number of calls during each of those time segments.

The chart system forces us to deal with issues quantitatively rather than emotionally. The evidence from our charts will not let us kid ourselves about our efforts and progress. We can't deceive ourselves into thinking that we're really trying to lose weight when our charts clearly show us that our intake of calories and fat grams is still sky high. We can't honestly tell ourselves that we're really trying to get ahead in our careers when our charts tell us that we haven't been putting in more time or doing anything else we know we need to do to make our goals a reality.

For me, a chart is like a corporate balance sheet. I know exactly what I need to do each and every day to reach my goals. Charts leave no room for doubt, argument, excuses, or self-deception. We can always see where we are, where we've been, what we've done, and what we need to do next. We can always see the "big picture."

The chart system has also helped me have a more long-term perspective, and to realize that what I do today directly affects what will happen to me in the future.

The system has worked for me, and I know it can work for you. Take some time to transform your goals into chart form. Then put the charts up where you can't possibly miss them – in your office, or in the kitchen or bathroom. Take control of your future by tracking your progress today!

(Refer to the next sections for specific examples of charts.)

Remember:
•   Start to chart!

Door-to-Door Success

When I was 20, I was offered an opportunity to sell vinyl siding door-to-door. I had only been earning about $18,000 a year working with my father in the insurance business. I was told that salesmen my age in the siding company were earning twice that amount. So I joined up with this company to see what they were doing to be able to make so much money at such a young age.

On my first day, the weather was 20 degrees below zero with the wind chill factor. I made up my mind that if the other salesmen could do it, so could I. I went out door-to-door with one of the other salesmen, and though I didn't know all the terms, and didn't understand the products very well, I wanted desperately to increase my income, and I felt I was teachable.

I learned an invaluable lesson from the owner of the company, who was also my father-in-law and mentor. He used a specific technique to ensure success – a special system for selling door-to-door. He had perfected it by knocking on many thousands of doors himself. He learned what to say, how to say it, and how to keep track of the entire process.

The system worked for anyone who used it. There was no risk and no investment. The entire program had already been established, tried, and tested. Using the system, I saw my income quadruple during my first year with him.

The element of the business that was unique was the actual tracking system he had developed. This system of tracking, which he called the "chart system," proved to be the key element of success in his company. His salespeople knew exactly what needed to be done to make money. They knew that if they followed their charts, they could and would make money.

The chart I've included at the end of this section is an

example of what the salespeople used in that business.

Referring to this chart, let's discuss how the charting method works when applied to the door-to-door sales business. In column 1 of the sales chart, the salespeople logged the day of the week; in column 2, the number of doors they knocked on that day; in column 3, the number of people they talked to; in column 4, the number of follow-up appointments they set up; in column 5, the number of actual sales presentations they made; in column 6, the number of orders taken or sales made; and in column 7, the amount of money they made from their activity that week.

If someone complained about not making enough money, all the manager had to do was look at his or her charts.

It was all there in black and white.

In that business, it was already established that if a salesperson knocked on 75 doors a day, he would talk to 25 people, make five appointments, make three presentations, and get one sale. If he did this five days a week, he'd have five sales – two of which would be approved for financing. That meant that he would make a minimum of $500 per week. If he didn't make at least that much money, he could look at his charts and immediately determine what he was doing wrong – whether he was not knocking on enough doors or not setting up enough presentations. Whatever it was, he could see the imbalance and begin working immediately to correct it.

These charts were kept up on a wall for everyone to see. This was an excellent enhancement to the system because it provided even more motivation for each salesperson.

I have adapted these charts to fit my current business dealings as well as my personal life. I still make a habit of putting the charts up in a visible location in my office and at home. The charts serve as an ever-present reminder of how and what I need to do each day to achieve my goals.

Remember:
* Charting creates financial focus.

DAY	HITS	TALK	APTS	PITCH	SALES	$
1						
2						
3						
4						
5						
6						
7						

Weight Less

As I've already said, charts can be used in virtually any area of our personal lives to efficiently attain our goals. One example of this is when I used charts for weight loss.

I've included this chart at the end of this section. Please refer to it as we discuss how it works. In column 1 of the chart, I listed the day of the week; in column 2, a list of food I consumed; in column 3, the exercise I did that day; in column 4, my current weight; and in column 5, my goal weight. (My goal weight was not my ultimate goal, but my goal for the day or for that week.)

When I started keeping a weight-loss chart, I weighed 240 pounds. My goal was 200 pounds. I figured I could, realistically, lose two pounds per week, so I set up my chart as follows for the first week:

1st day	Actual _____	Goal 240
2nd day	Actual _____	Goal 240
3rd day	Actual _____	Goal 239
4th day	Actual _____	Goal 239
5th day	Actual _____	Goal 239
6th day	Actual _____	Goal 239
7th day	Actual _____	Goal 238

Instead of looking at my ultimate goal of 200 pounds every day, I'd see what my goal was for that day. Just as Alcoholics Anonymous teaches its participants to go "one day at a time," so I taught myself to lose weight one day at a time.

I was able to "see" success every day. It was much easier and simpler for me to keep on track if I concentrated on a single day at a time and took little bites out of the big goal. I saw my goal actualizing right in front of me every day. I experienced tiny successes continuously.

There's nothing that motivates people more than achieving success, even if it comes just a little bit at a time.

Remember:
• By helping us focus, charting promotes success.

DAY	FOOD	EXERCISE	ACTUAL	GOAL

Personal Charting

There are many things in my life that I want to make certain I do on a regular basis.

I've included another chart at the end of this section – one that I currently use. This is an example of the kind of chart on which you can track more than one objective.

Across the top of the chart (on line 1) I put the day of the week or the date. On line 2 I fill in the time I got up. On line 3 is a place to check whether I had prayer in the morning and evening. Line 4 is for affirmations, and line 5 is for exercise. I chart my water intake on line 6, and scripture reading on line 7. Line 8 tracks whether I wrote in my journal that day, and line 9 is for my reading goal. On line 10 I enter the time I stopped eating at night, and on line 11, the time I went to bed.

These are just a few of the many activities that can be quantitatively charted. And they *should* be charted if we're trying to improve ourselves in any of these areas. It's important to measure our progress toward our goals.

For example, I had a goal to get up earlier – at 6 a.m. – so I decided to start tracking the exact time I got up every day on a chart. I listed the time, and at the end of the week, it was easy to evaluate my level of success.

I knew how easy it would be to let the goal slide if I didn't do this. The fact is, as human beings, we have a tendency to fool ourselves into thinking we're making progress when we aren't. We often overlook, make excuses, and rationalize. But I knew that once I started charting the time I woke up each morning, I would have to deal with the cold, hard reality.

Charts won't let me fool myself. It keeps the truth right in front of me. All that matters to my chart is whether I did or didn't get up at 6 a.m.

I also wanted to make sure I had prayer in the mornings and evenings. I wanted to make this a habit, so I included a place on my chart for prayer, and I simply indicated "Yes" or a "No." The same with affirmations. Did I say them each day? I'd write "Yes" or "No." Did I exercise? "Yes" or "No." If I exercised, what kind did I do? I'd write the activity in the box. How much water did I drink? I'd write "high," "medium," or "low," depending on the amount. In order to stay healthy, I knew I had to drink large amounts of water each day, and my chart showed me whether or not I was actually doing it.

Did I read scriptures that day? Again, "Yes" or "No." Did I write in my journal that day? Did I read that day? What time did I stop eating? Finally, I entered the last item on my chart: the time I went to bed. All this information went onto my chart.

I could even refer to this information to help me figure out what was happening in other areas of my life that I was tracking on other charts. On my weight chart, for example, if I wasn't where I wanted to be at the end of the week, I could look at my activities and see what was wrong. The chart usually showed me that I hadn't succeeded in losing the two pounds that week because I was eating too late at night. I discovered, through charting, that it mattered less *how much* I ate, and more *when* I ate – a very helpful piece of information.

Overall, this simple but powerful system has helped me to be a successful goal-achiever by taking action and receiving rewards, step-by-step. It has enabled me to keep things in perspective. It has also helped me not to fool myself into thinking I'm making progress when I'm really not. Putting everything in simple black and white serves as an ongoing balance and "reality check."

The chart system has worked and continues to work for me. It gives me the control over my life that I want. It helps me act, rather than react, and control my activities rather than be controlled by them.

I challenge you to put charts to use in your life today and watch yourself finally begin to move in the direction you want to go.

Remember:
- Charting provides a "reality check" for daily living.
- Make a list of five things you want to get done each day, and chart them.

note: please write to us for your personal copy

Key 8:

EXERCISING OUR MINDS

A *Little* Learning
Can Be a Dangerous Thing

The more we learn, the more we should realize how little we know. The more we know, the more humble we should become as we realize how little we know compared to the vast quantity of universal knowledge that actually exists.

It's like the young man who has never left the small valley where he was born. He thinks he knows everything there is to know. But the minute he climbs to the ridge of the mountain overlooking the valley and sees far-reaching vistas of plains, rivers, valleys, and mountain ranges, his horizons suddenly expand and he realizes that his knowledge encompasses only a tiny corner of a vast universe.

This is exactly what happens to us as we begin to climb out of our valleys of ignorance. New and exciting worlds of knowledge unfold before us as we move higher.

After graduating from high school or college, most people allow their acquisition of knowledge to slow to a snail's pace, or to stop altogether. They might take a vocational class or a job-related seminar or two, but the amount of time and energy they devote to broadening their minds is typically very limited.

Let's not make this same mistake. We must continue to "feed" our minds. We should continue to learn throughout our lives. It's vitally important! Our intelligence level is directly impacted by the amount of knowledge we acquire.

We all have a responsibility to ourselves to acquire knowledge – even little bits of knowledge – on an ongoing basis. I try to learn something new every day. If we do this we can feel good about ourselves at the end of each day. It creates a great feeling of success and personal advancement. Whenever I read or hear or discover something new, I say to myself, "I learned something new today!" I use that as a verbal confirmation to myself.

Orison Swett Marden said, "The belief was general among the ancient Greeks, that the secret of eternal youth is to always be learning something new." If we don't learn something new during the day, then we should ask someone about something we don't know, or look up a new word in the dictionary. We'll be more knowledgeable, better informed, more prepared for success, and – who knows? – we might even achieve an eternally youthful mind!

Remember:
- Make it a point to acquire some piece of knowledge every day.

Read On

As I mentioned earlier, I was blessed to have found a mentor early in my career (my father-in-law) – at the age of 20. At the time I met him I'd only read two books: *The Fox Family* and *The Red Car.*

He taught me the value of reading. He is one of the wealthiest men in America. One of his keys to success was to read everything he could get his hands on. Even though he had no formal education beyond the sixth grade, he was totally self-educated in all aspects of life.

And it was all through reading.

Our knowledge is directly related to how much and what we read. Reading is an incredible source of intellectual expansion. The more we read, the better we'll be able to converse with and relate to people from all walks of life. This makes us more likely to succeed in our careers, and more enjoyable to our friends – not to mention the personal satisfaction we'll get out of gaining a more thorough and diverse base of knowledge.

Want to know more? Read more.

Want to read more? Start small.

Begin by reading about 15 minutes a day. Don't grab a 500-page novel and try to finish it this week. Make reading enjoyable. Get used to the activity in small segments, just like starting an exercise program. You'd never try to jump right into a running schedule of 20 miles a day, would you? The same logic applies to starting a reading program.

We need to start small and build up to a comfortable level that we'll be happy with. This will help us make reading a lifetime habit.

We should look for five- and ten-minute segments of time

to read. There are lots of empty niches: in the bathroom, at the doctor's or dentist's office, waiting for a business appointment, standing in line at the grocery store, or eating lunch.

We should keep a book nearby all the time. This will allow us to do more reading, and will also subconsciously encourage us to read more often. Whenever a spare minute becomes available, we can open up the book and read. We'll be more productive with our time and eliminate the frustration of having to spend five minutes here and ten minutes there unproductively waiting.

What should we read? We could start with a newspaper – the sections we're most interested in. I suggest *USA Today*. The stories are quick-reading and informative. Then try *Reader's Digest*. It features short, fun, and exciting articles of general interest to all. Magazines like *Success* and *Entrepreneur* carry stories about individuals who started from nothing and built remarkable businesses.

When it comes to fiction, it is very important to stay away from trash. The majority of the books on supermarket racks aren't worth our valuable time. We should find good, enjoyable authors. And we shouldn't be afraid to read the classics. Some of the classics might seem intimidating and dry, but they are really some of the most entertaining books available. Think about it – how does a classic become a classic? The answer is simple: because people like us have been reading it and enjoying it and telling their friends about it for decades or maybe even centuries.

In contrast, few of the paperbacks on the racks in grocery and convenience stores today will be in print two years from now. (Some will go out of print even before the bananas in the produce section turn brown.) Libraries and bookstores are much better hunting grounds for good literature.

Reading can be a source of knowledge, recreation, motivation, and inspiration. Fall in love with it. I did, and it made all the difference in my life.

Remember:
- Always carry a book.
- Reading leads to intelligence.

Book Store Joy

We should go to a book store every few months and purchase a half dozen books or so on a variety of subjects to stay educated and informed. I suggest books on the subjects of motivation, psychology, marketing, advertising, and business. These are the areas that interest me and touch my life closely and most often. Reading these books allows me to maintain an edge of expertise in my life.

I buy books that interest me on other subjects, too. They help broaden my horizons and round out my education.

If you don't want to or can't purchase books regularly, then utilize the local library. A wealth of information is contained inside those walls ... and the price is right!

Remember:
- Read about things that are of personal interest.

The Blind Builder

No contractor would start building a house without first having a set of plans or blueprints to guide him. To do so would be to build blindly. No surgeon would grab a scalpel and perform surgery without first studying the patient's charts, X-rays, and any other information that would help him know exactly where he needed to cut and what he needed to accomplish.

And yet, crazy as it may sound, most people live their lives blindly, without a plan. They don't make the effort to get the information and knowledge they need to help them live "intentionally" (as Thoreau put it).

Let's strive to find out more about everything that touches us. We need to learn all we can about specific subjects prior to experiencing them. We should work to become experts in all our endeavors and in the various aspects of our lives.

Before I became a father, I read all I could about child-rearing. Before I purchased a vehicle, I read and found out about the best cars with respect to my needs. Before I moved to a new city, I researched all the cities and towns in the United States. Before I started investing in real estate, I read books, studied business plans, researched marketing ideas, and attended many seminars. I did the same thing in the area of personal development.

Before I ever took the first actual step in these endeavors, I researched what I was doing. I tried to be ahead of the game, and things turned out much better than they would have if I had charged in blindly. Spending time researching things puts money in our pockets. We are more likely to make wise decisions and less likely to make costly mistakes.

Let's not limit our research and studies only to the areas of life in which we are involved, or planning to be involved. We should strive to acquire as much knowledge as we can in a wide spectrum of areas. According to William Lynn Phelps, "People of tremendous mental vitality are intensely interested in a variety of things." We should read magazines and books, ask questions, and explore. It will make us more well-rounded individuals, and could open our eyes to exciting new facets of life.

Remember:
- "Read before you leap."
- Research increases the probability of success.

Why Reinvent the Wheel?

Why repeat the same mistakes others have made? Why start from scratch, again and again? Why experiment and endure trial and error to discover the formulas that have already been established?

We can learn from the experiences of others.

An important part of education is to learn the lessons offered by those who have gone before. I love to listen to people who have walked life's path and learned perspectives that can help me with my own challenges and goals. By doing this, we can avoid having to start from the beginning – having to learn how to sit up, then crawl, and finally walk before we run. We can learn from the experience of others and compress the process.

Imagine trying to learn how to use a computer program without a manual, or without having someone help us that knows how to do it. Imagine trying to assemble a complicated machine or appliance without the instructions! Life is the same way: we need to pay attention to the "instructions" of the people who have already successfully put the pieces together.

Remember:
- Value and learn from the experiences of others.

Creating Our Own Positive World

One of the most profound choices we face is deciding what kind of a world we want to create for ourselves. The vast majority of people live in a world that is negative, limited, difficult, frightening, threatening, confining, and ugly.

My challenge to us all is to create a positive, bright, happy world for ourselves and for others.

"Wait a minute!" you're probably thinking. "The world is what it is no matter what I do. I can't create it. It's already there."

Yes, it *is* already there. But there's the good as well as the bad, the beautiful as well as the ugly, the love as well as the fear. That's the point: it's *all* there.

It's up to us to choose which perspective we will take. Will we, like many people, choose to focus on the dark side? Or will we decide to concentrate on the bright side? Like the glass that's half empty and half full, both viewpoints are equally real. It's simply a question of which vantage point we choose to take.

That decision will dictate the kind of world we "create" for ourselves, the kind of energy and attitude that surrounds us, and the kinds of people and circumstances we attract into our lives.

The half-empty or half-full glass example may seem trivial, but when we put the principle to work, the world changes before our eyes. This has certainly proven to be true in my own life.

For example, I lost a business in New York years ago. When I analyze it, however, there were many positive aspects to it. I was moving to Atlanta, and it saved me having to fly back and forth. Maybe someone would have done something wrong since I wouldn't be there all the time supervising, and I would have been named in a big lawsuit. Or maybe I would have stayed in that business the rest of my life and never written this book or actualized my full potential.

I was also arrested and spent a few days in jail because of ludicrous charges that, when they finally came to court, were thrown out by the judge. But if I hadn't had that experience, I wouldn't be able to relate to inmates, and wouldn't have started the Inside Corporation to help them. The experience helped me develop patience, and taught me the value of true friends, as well as many other valuable lessons that have helped me ever since.

Because of these experiences, I also found myself with no credit. But even having no credit was a blessing. Why? Because it taught me to be creative, and get what I needed without credit. This has helped me in business ever since, giving me an advantage over those who have not had to develop financial creativity. It was also a big lesson in humility, which is extremely valuable in the business world.

I had to start completely over, both in my personal and business life. While this was a painful experience, I realize that it was one of the most valuable experiences in my entire life, because it gave me the self-confidence to know that I can land on my feet after a hard fall.

Clearly, it's important to create a positive world – to overcome the negative thinking that surrounds us and focus on the positives rather than the negatives. But how do we go about it?

One way is to fill our minds with positive books, tapes, videos, seminars, lectures, and other supportive materials. Surveys of the wealthiest people in the world show that most of them listen to positive motivational tapes frequently. My computer friends have a saying: "Garbage in, garbage out." It's so true! If we only feed our minds the typical negative "garbage" that is everywhere in our society, that's exactly what will be manifest in our lives. But if we stuff our minds with thoughts that are good and positive, good and positive things will then begin to happen.

Another way to create a positive world is to surround ourselves with positive people in a positive environment. In my business offices throughout the country, the atmosphere is quite different from the surrounding establishments. I made the commitment from the start to create a place of sanctity, where a feeling of trust and commonality was felt – a place of refuge from the negative influences of the world.

To do this, I knew I would have to hire good, positive people. I remember when I hired one of our administrative staff, over one hundred people applied for the job. After the first day of interviewing, I had already seen over 75 applicants. I had over 20 to go on the second day and in walked a woman that I immediately felt was right. I canceled all the other interviews, knowing she was the one.

She was the type of person people felt comfortable with immediately. She came across as competent, confident, and secure. She was friendly, compassionate, and intelligent. She radiated peace. She turned out to be even better than I expected. Maybe it was the belief and trust I gave her. Maybe it was the positive atmosphere in which she was able to let her true self shine forth. Maybe it was the responsibility that was given to her. Maybe it was all the above.

I feel I have succeeded in creating my own (actually, "our own") positive world in the workplace. I try to make sure that our work environment is a place of safety and security. Nothing negative is said – no sarcasm, no backbiting – only positivity, an uplifting belief in each other, and an atmosphere of creativity. This is the result of demanding goodness from everyone. I believe we all want to be good people. We all want to be positive, kind to others, uplifting in the way we act and the things we say and do. My part has been to make sure that everyone knows that this is what I want and that nothing less will do.

We can do this in our personal lives as well. We simply need to make a habit of spending time around positive people and staying away from the negative influences that abound. We need to read positive books, see positive movies, say positive things. We need to stay away from evil and negativity. I personally cannot tolerate negativity. If I hear it, I move away or shut it out. It literally makes me feel sick inside.

Repeated positive statements also help. I have heard that it takes 14 positive affirmations to overcome a negative. Here are some examples of the types of things we can say to ourselves in the form of regular affirmations:

"I am getting better every day in every way."

"I surround myself each day with positive experiences."

"I know that I am becoming the person I always dreamed possible."

"I expect good things to happen to me today. I deserve them."

"This day is going to be a wonderful day in my life."

I try to write out new affirmations every week or so and try to read them aloud each morning and evening. As we get more and more used to this activity, our affirmations will become more detailed, and they will begin to dramatically affect everything we do, think, and say.

We must also be on guard to protect ourselves against the pernicious effects of complaining. Everyone has problems, concerns, and challenges. Life is about how we deal with them. Are we paralyzed by our problems, or do we adopt a healthy perspective about them and accept them as challenges, maintaining a positive attitude in spite of them? We can't have this healthy attitude if we complain about our challenges. We should think of every complaint we make – either spoken or unspoken – as an immediate withdrawal from our emotional bank accounts. Complaining is a big negative – it simply doesn't do any good, only bad. Sarcasm and other types of negative thinking fall into the same category. There are a lot of things in our lives that we can't control, but we *are* in control of whether or not we indulge in these self-destructive thought patterns and behaviors. We should leap at the chance to control this aspect of our lives, and make ourselves better and happier *now*.

Of course, all of this is easier said than done, but nothing good comes easy. It takes practice. We need to make it a constant part of our lives. When we do, we will see stunning results as our lives literally transform themselves and we become surrounded by the wonderful world we have created.

Remember:

- Exude positivism in every area of life.

Key 9:

TAPPING INTO PEOPLE POWER

Networking Magic

We can't reach the top alone. And we can't get rich by ourselves. Even if we could, who would want to?

The fact is, people are what life is all about. People make our lives worth living. And when we work to develop sustaining, long-term, mutually beneficial relationships, people will help us reach our goals – including our financial goals.

Networking is a powerful tool that helps us reach higher levels of success by getting out and meeting, knowing, and spending time with others. Simply stated, people like to do business with people they know and feel comfortable with. Networking, in its purest business definition, means the exchange of information among individuals or groups of individuals. We can utilize this dynamic tool to advance our careers and businesses, while at the same time helping those in our networks do the same.

For example, if you owned a car repair business and I was in the insurance business, we could refer people back and forth to each other. There are networking clubs designed for the primary purpose of gathering people together so they can meet each other in the pursuit of mutually beneficial relationships.

Networking has become a popular concept in recent years, but few people do it right. They rarely get beyond the superficial level of introductions. They fail to take the necessary step of actually pursuing and building relationships with other individuals. This isn't easy for most people, even though they know it's worth the effort.

Then how do we go about networking? The first step is to take the initiative. Making friends and developing relationships requires effort. We should get out and meet people, be outgoing, and find things we have in common with the people we come in contact with. Granted, we won't be able to (or want to) pursue relationships with *everyone* we meet, but unless we go through this initial process, we won't find the people we *do* want to get to know.

We should keep the business cards of all the people we meet. It's a good idea to start a Rolodex or other type of record-keeping system with this information, recording the dates and places where we met and any other descriptive details we can think of.

It's very worthwhile to read Harvey MacKay's books: *Swim With The Sharks Without Being Eaten Alive* and *Beware The Naked Man Who Offers You His Shirt*. In these excellent books, he offers some valuable tips on the art of keeping track of the individuals we meet and the true value of this practice.

I can testify to the value of networking. It has been a source of personal and financial fulfillment in my own life.

For example, a business acquaintance and I used to go to lunch every month or so. His name was Carlos Rivera. He was a real estate agent and a good friend – a good friend because we made an effort to develop a relationship with each another.

Carlos had a master's degree in marketing and was an exceptional real estate agent. He never pressured people. He was a true professional. I sent him business and vice versa. We respected each other and enjoyed the association. That relationship resulted in substantial additional business for both of us over the years. Fostering and maintaining that relationship put thousands of dollars in each of our pockets.

The key to making these types of relationships work is periodic maintenance. We must work to maintain any relationship, even if we just call, write, or see each other every month or so.

While at a business luncheon, my wife and I sat next to a gentleman named David. We started up a casual conversation. We took the initiative and found out things about Dave, including what we had in common.

Since that day we've gone boating, waterskiing, and have

played racquetball together. I was able to attend and speak at one of the business organizations to which he belongs. All this came from simply saying hello, taking the initiative to get to know someone we met at a luncheon, and making the effort to develop a relationship.

It's important to understand that our purpose for being friendly wasn't to add another name to our network for the purpose of financial benefits – it was to establish a genuine friendship. When we approach networking with sincerity and the desire not only to *have* good friends, but to *be* a good friend, the material benefits will follow naturally.

Networking doesn't have to be done face-to-face. It can be done on a long-distance basis with people we never physically meet. Before I moved from New York to Atlanta, everything in my life had blown up in my face. I had to start over from scratch. I couldn't even afford to pay rent.

But I got a break through networking. A friend of mine had a business associate living in Bermuda, who traded some property in Bermuda for a 5,000-square-foot, $750,000 home in Atlanta, located one mile from the governor's mansion.

I drove by the house and saw that this huge home was overgrown and unkept. I decided to take photos of the house and fax them to the owner in Bermuda. I wrote a letter explaining who I was and describing my experience in real estate. I worked hard with phone calls and correspondence to establish a relationship with this gentleman.

To compress this story, I wound up living in that mansion for almost three years ... free! The new owner didn't want to leave the house empty any longer while he was trying to sell it. He felt comfortable with me, he liked the way I presented myself, and he appreciated the initiative I took in establishing a relationship with him.

This was a great blessing at that point in my life. And the benefit was more than financial. Living in the mansion enabled me to see myself living at my previous level. It helped me to visualize success and envision a fast return to my former income level.

Someone once said that a relationship is like a solid, long-term investment. There is an initial outlay, and small subsequent "payments" to be made. But when properly managed and maintained, it will continue to produce profitable dividends for us throughout our lifetimes.

Take this advice to heart. Invest in the longest-lasting and most profitable commodity in the world: relationships.

Remember:
•   All around us are relationships waiting to happen.

Our Most Important Relationships

As I've said before, I'm a big believer in living a balanced life. Well, there was a time when I was out of balance. I was so busy making money and trying to get ahead that I neglected the one thing that makes life worth living: relationships.

No matter what kind of success we achieve in the business world, it won't compare to the joy of having good friends. I believe that a lot of people confuse the word "friend" with "acquaintance." To me, a friend is someone you can call at three in the morning and know they'll come over and help you if you really need it without hesitation. A friend is someone who will love and accept you unconditionally, even though they don't always agree with what you think or how you behave. Getting together with these special people, enjoying their company, watching their families grow ... this is a facet of life that business successes can never replace.

Our most important relationships are those within our own homes – with our spouse and children. A great prophet once said, "No success can compensate for failure in the home." Nothing could be more true.

I'd like to share an excellent technique I have used for building strong family relationships through communication. It's a technique that will open up the paths of communication between you and the members of your family, and will allow everyone to vent any pent-up negative feelings they might be harboring.

Here's how it's done: at least once a month, take time to have a one-on-one "interview" with every member of your family – including your spouse. You can make this a formal, sit-down interview in your office, or an informal chat on the way to a ballet lesson or baseball game – whichever is most effective.

Some individuals like the formality. It makes the event more meaningful. Others will be put off or intimidated by a formal interview. You need to judge what works best for each member of the family.

Let's say the family member you're interviewing is a 16-year-old daughter. This is a time to ask her some questions that she can answer freely and without interruption, condemnation, or condescension. You should ask what you can do to make her life more enjoyable and fulfilled, and what you can do that will help her achieve her goals. Ask about her friends, how high school is going, and if anything is bothering her at school, at home, or at her part-time job at the supermarket. And don't forget to ask if *you* are doing anything that bothers her.

Then reverse the process, and let her interview you.

It's important to follow the rules of the game, however. The main rule is this: after asking each question, you must listen and not respond. This means that you can't react with words, sounds, gestures, body language, or facial expressions. She must know that she won't be interrupted so she can freely say what's on her mind without fearing judgement or rebuke. The same rules apply when she asks you the questions.

You should take notes on what is discussed in order to work on the list. These notes can be kept in a notebook or planner, and reviewed every week until the next interview. Then, as the first part of the next interview, you simply get out your list and review the notes with her.

When a husband and wife have an interview, they should take turns asking and answering questions, and let each other know when they are finished. Only then should they move on to the next question.

One of the spouses (let's say the husband) should ask a question like: "What can I do to enhance our marriage?" He should then sit and listen for as long as his wife responds, giving her his undivided attention without responding in any way – even with his posture. If she needs to think about her answer and has to sit there quietly for some time, that's okay. He should wait, giving her the time she needs. By doing this, he lets her know that he is really interested in how she feels.

Her answer may be something like, "I really enjoy our time when we get to go on dates. I want to go more often, and I want to go with just you – not with friends and family. Another thing you can do for me is give me enough time to get ready before we go to functions. I feel best when I'm not rushed, so I'd appreciate more notice so I have time to get ready without hurrying so much."

Of course, the answers will not always be as positive or gentle as that. There may be times when the responses are mean and cutting. But when that happens, at least the frustration or bitterness behind the response has been aired and is "out" where it can be dealt with. Too often, people let things build up inside them until they blow up – often over something small – and cause much more damage than if they had been handled before hitting the boiling point.

These personal interviews are a tremendous technique, and can help us uncover many things that can improve and enhance our relationships.

Another fun little family relationship-builder is a game called the "Ungame." This is another tool to open the lines of communication among family members. We can play it with friends – old and new friends, even acquaintances we want to get to know better. It's great for adults and older children. It can be found at most toy stores.

It's also a great idea to take the members of our immediate families out on "dates." These dates should be one-on-one – just the two of you. I try to take each of my children out on a date at least once a month, and my wife at least once a week.

Whatever tools or techniques we decide to use to build our most important relationships, the main point is to keep the channels of communication open and let the people around us know we care. Whatever efforts we make in this area will be amply rewarded throughout our lives.

Remember:
- Do something to improve every relationship you have.
- Try interviewing someone you love.

Acceptance and Understanding

I used to be angry at my father. I wanted him to be something that he was not. Undoubtedly, he wanted the same from me. This caused a huge separation between us that wasn't resolved until two weeks before he died. Looking back, I realize that our problem was not that we wanted each other to be different. Most people probably want the people closest to them to be different at least in some ways. No, our problem was that we did not understand and accept each other for the people we were.

Some parents I know didn't want their child to paint her room. Why? Some others didn't want their son to have a friend sleep over for two nights in a row? Why? One parent wouldn't let her child grow his hair long or pierce his ear. Why? If we control our children too tightly – especially over things that don't really matter – they will revolt and do something much worse.

The daughter of some friends of mine is a straight-A student and never gets in trouble. She wanted to get a tattoo. They said no. Then she turned 17 and wanted to express herself as her friends were doing. She again pleaded for the tattoo. "Absolutely not!" was her answer. Not long after, she showed up with a huge tattoo that covered most of her back! Now what? I believe that if her parents had discussed it with her, and explained more fully how they felt and why, and if they had really tried to understand her and accept her feelings about the tattoo, she would have first tried a small tattoo in an inconspicuous place, and it probably would have stopped there. Instead, in her desire to express herself and prove that it was her body and that she could do what she wanted with it, she made a huge and permanent "statement."

Lies and withheld truths flourish in the absence of understanding and acceptance. They also thrive when someone fears that they won't be understood and accepted. It's best – always best – to tell it like it is and let the chips fall where they may.

Let's set the stage for understanding and acceptance in our relationships by *being* understanding and accepting. People will be more honest and open with us, and will return the favor by accepting us right back.

Remember:
*   Understand and accept people.
*   Be honest and open and expect acceptance from others.

Simple Gestures

Sometimes it's the simplest, littlest things that produce the greatest rewards. Nowhere is this more true than in the area of relationship building.

During one of my trips, I found myself out of state and needing to do some wire transfers to and from my checking account. I was a fairly new customer of this bank and needed some special assistance. The woman at the bank I contacted by phone – Heidi – was very friendly and helpful. Even though we'd never met, she provided me with superb service. She was friendly, efficient, concerned about my needs, and went out of her way to be helpful.

I was so impressed and grateful that I sent her flowers afterwards just to say thanks.

When I returned home, I went to the bank to make some deposits. The teller who was helping me looked at the name on my deposit ticket and said, "I know who you are! You're the guy who sent flowers to Heidi, aren't you?" She went and got Heidi, who happened to be the head bank teller, from her office. She was so thrilled and surprised to receive the flowers that she had told everyone about them. She and the flowers were the talk of the bank for days.

From that moment on I enjoyed personal, friendly, preferential treatment, quick service, and many other benefits. Heidi and the rest of the bank staff made my banking life very simple and smooth. I didn't have to go through the typical red tape you run into at most financial institutions.

Through my relationship with Heidi, I in turn met and developed a personal and professional relationship with the manager, executive vice-president, and the regional manager of the bank. I moved all of my banking business there and have also done corporate executive training for some of the executive staff and branch managers.

This is how a simple gesture can lead to a relationship that will blossom and multiply in ways we can't begin to imagine! I could never have foreseen the value that came from sending those flowers. That simple act of appreciation opened the door to great service and a series of wonderful long-term relationships.

Of course, we don't always have to send flowers to show our gratitude. Simple "thank you" letters can work miracles, too. One good suggestion is to write "thank you" letters to anyone who does something nice for us, has taken time with us, has had us over for dinner, or has just generally touched our lives in some way. This applies to anyone – from acquaintances to close friends. And we mustn't forget family members. We should let these people know we appreciate them and all that they do for us. It's important to let them know that they are an important and irreplaceable part of our lives.

Whenever I have an appointment with someone, visit a friend, have a get-together, or anything else along those lines, I try to send letters of appreciation. Anytime someone does something for me that they didn't have to do, I try to acknowledge the act in writing. People feel wonderful when they receive a letter that expresses thanks for something they've done.

Unfortunately, most people never take the time to show their appreciation in writing. They are missing out on an opportunity to build long-lasting relationships – an opportunity that would yield rich rewards in both their personal and business lives.

There is an old adage, "A picture is worth a thousand words." Well, I testify that "A group of kind words is worth a thousand actions."

There's a photo finishing store that I used to frequent. It's run by a family – a father, mother, and daughter. They were always so friendly and professional that one day I felt compelled to take the time to write and send them a "thank you" letter.

The next time I visited their store, they not only thanked me for the letter, but I saw that they had laminated it onto the top of the front counter for everyone to see. The service they were providing was exceptional already, but it actually improved after the letter.

I often have photos reproduced in various sizes for promotional purposes. I went to pick up my prints one day and the father had made several different sizes of master negatives for me, and didn't charge me a penny for them.

On another occasion I had ordered reprints that required special handling by an outside lab. They were promised to me the next day at noon. When I called, the pictures weren't there yet, so the owner's wife got into her car, drove to the lab, and personally picked them up for me.

Another simple relationship-building gesture is to be genuinely concerned about the people we know and meet, and express that concern. One of the best ways to do that is to simply take the time to listen to them.

I used to really love yogurt. There used to be a yogurt store just a few blocks away from my home. Whenever I stopped by, I took the time to talk to the manager and to be genuinely friendly. This man would talk to me about famous people that came into the shop and about what was happening in his personal life. I wouldn't talk for more than a minute or two each visit, but he appreciated me and the attention I gave him, and he went overboard to show it.

I always try to ask for discounts wherever I go, and the yogurt store was no exception. The manager was more than happy to give me a coupon for 1/2 off this visit and the next as well. This went on for the next two or three visits, and then he started giving me the discount automatically even without a coupon.

Later, I had a garage sale and he happened to show up. I half jokingly asked him if he had any coupons left. He went back to the store and brought back 30 free coupons!

I was the recipient of his generosity because I time to

carry out the simple act of listening and showing genuine concern. It's just one more example of how treating people right and establishing relationships can pay off in dividends that are immeasurable, unexpected, and unending.

Remember:
- A simple gesture can take us a long way.
- Always remember to thank others.

Good Service Means Good Business

Whatever businesses or careers we're in, we can increase our incomes by giving our customers or clients better service.

If we look around, we don't have to look far to see examples of businesses that are suffering because they don't give people the kind of service they deserve and want.

Take movie theaters, for example. What business are they in? It's not entertainment. Seventy-five percent of the gross ticket price goes to the movie company. They are in the business of concessions. (Sounds like politics!) They make their money by selling popcorn, drinks, candy, and other treats. They use movies to get people in the doors, and once they're in, they sell them exorbitantly priced treats. When I estimated how much theaters charge for these treats – about $40 per gallon for soft drinks (which cost them about 25¢), and about $900 per pound for popcorn.

With that kind of profit margin, I don't understand why theaters don't give their customers better service. Why don't they have more people behind the counters? A lot of people don't buy treats at theaters simply because there always seems to be too long of a line. Why don't they have employees selling treats up and down the aisles before the movie? And why don't they have a brief intermission in the middle of movies, like they used to, to give people a chance to buy more treats and visit the restroom?

What about dry cleaners? The people who work in these establishments should remember their customers' names, and give discounts by giving coupons and honoring competitors' coupons. They should always give their regular customers the discounted prices even without coupons. And what about claim tickets? Everyone loses them anyway. Why do they hassle their customers by asking them to keep track of claim tickets? They should know them and make it easy for them. Pick up and delivery is another service that dry cleaners should offer if they're committed to giving good service. These are things people want, but don't get very often, if at all.

Simply stated, business people and professionals should treat their customers like kings, and should really act like they believe the old saying, "The customer is always right." We shouldn't have to use our negotiating skills to get what we want.

Case in point: a new video store opened in our neighborhood, and a huge sign proclaimed that if you wanted a new release, and it was not in, you would get a rain check to rent that movie free the next time you came in. The management's thinking was obviously that you would rent other movies and come back later for the free one. The gimmick worked. The store was packed.

However, the management must have stopping thinking after the initial brainstorming session. I asked what would happen if we came back and the movie we had a free rain check for was out again. The correct answer should have been, "Then we'll give you another movie free to compensate for your frustration." But that's not the answer I got. I was told that there was no policy for coming back if the guaranteed movie was not there on a return visit.

To make matters worse, I tried to check out four new releases since two of the movies I wanted to rent were out, even though they were "guaranteed." I was told that I could only rent two new releases during my first visit to the store, three my second visit, and four only after spending $100 there. I was with kids, and they wanted the four movies. So I decided to open two accounts – one in my name and the other in my son's name. But my son didn't have his license with him, and they needed a license, not just a credit card, to open an account. Then I told them I was going to rent a movie for $1.50 and immediately return it. That would mean that it would be my second time, and I would at least be able to get three new releases.

By the time they set up my account and I left, I felt like I had been through the wringer for an hour. I was frustrated and annoyed by the way I was treated by 16-year-old employees, and resented having to pay a $1.50 "bribe" to rent three movies instead of two, when I really wanted four, and when only two were the movies we originally wanted.

Let's not make these same types of mistakes in our own businesses or careers. Today more than ever, good service means good business. By treating our customers or clients like royalty, and letting them know that we value them, we're taking a giant step forward in insuring our own lasting success.

Remember:
- Ensure success by giving the best service.

"Honestly!"

We should never say the word "honestly." There's no reason to utter this word if we always speak honestly anyway.

A lot of people preface or end statements by saying, "honestly," "believe me," or "to tell you the truth." When they use these words and phrases, are we to assume that they are not being honest with us the rest of the time?

An indispensable key to successful relationships with people is honesty. If all our statements are honest anyway, there should be no need to clarify a specific statement by using a word like "honestly."

If we do, how will anyone know if we're telling the truth when we *don't* say it?

Remember:
* Speak straight, without prefaces.

When It's Not Worth the Fight

Face it: some things are worth fighting over; some aren't.

When someone cuts us off while driving on the freeway, what should we do? In the old days, I would have retaliated somehow. But that kind of behavior got me into uncomfortable situations more than once. I've changed. Now I try to let those sorts of things go. Why should we get angry and get our blood pressure up? Why should we let other people control our emotions and make us stoop to their level of behavior? Besides, nowadays you can get shot for that sort of thing.

When we order a salad with a meal and the waitress doesn't bring it when the meal is served, what should we do? Should we get mad at her for forgetting the salad? If we do, she might say we didn't order one, and then we're in an argument. Why not just say, "I'm sorry, could I have a salad please?" The key here is to understand that we don't have to prove anything to anyone. We just want our salad – not a fight.

We all find ourselves in situations where we're right and the other party is wrong. What should we do when that happens? If it's not worth a fight – and few things are – let's just let it go and get our salad. Anger is extremely stressful. Avoid it.

Remember:
• If it's not worth a fight, stay cool.

Key 10:

CULTIVATING CREATIVITY

Chalk Dot Mentality

We all have fertile minds that are waiting to be tilled and harvested. All we need are the tools.

Read Roger von Oech's books, *A Whack on the Side of the Head,* and *A Kick in the Seat of the Pants.* They're two of the most inspiring and insightful books into the world of creativity that I've read. He teaches us that child-like thinking will help us be creative in a way we once knew how to be, but have forgotten. He says that our school systems teach us not to be creative, but rather to fit routine, complacent molds. He challenges us, as adults, to strive to regain and nurture that fresh, child-like perspective and carefree spirit that is deep inside us.

Roger von Oech gives an example of the power and also the limitations of our minds. Two rooms are filled with people. One room is filled with grade school children between the ages of six and ten, and the other is filled with adults. The teacher walks up to the blackboard, draws a tiny, solid circle with chalk, and asks, "What is that?"

The question is asked to each group independently. The adult class looks at the teacher and agrees unanimously, "It's a chalk dot!" All the while they were thinking to themselves, "What is the meaning of such a silly question?"

The grade school class had a much different response. The children raised their hands. Each had a different answer. One said, "It's a marshmallow." Another said, "It's a snowflake." One even said, "Oh that's easy. It's the top of a telephone pole, looking down from an airplane!"

Think of the mind that came up with the telephone pole answer. Picture exactly what that child must have seen in his mind. Just think what the potential is for a mind like that in the marketing world, or as an inventor, or in any business!

I love that story. It brings to mind two questions: first, where does our creativity go; second, how can we get it back?

What a dramatic difference between the two groups! The adults didn't have to think about anything. They thought they knew exactly what the chalk dot was and weren't going to waste time or mental effort to think any further. But the children's minds were naturally open to creativity, wonder, and different ideas. Consequently, they came up with many amazing answers.

But the fact is, we *all* have that kind of creativity sleeping within us right now! Our challenge is to wake it up and let it come alive again in our adult minds.

Remember:
• Reawaken your childhood creativity.

Reviving Our Creative Minds

In our efforts to recapture the creativity we had as children, we can't go back in time and start over. We can, however, realize how our lives have molded us, and work to revive our natural creativity and individuality.

We've been taught in most school systems that there's only one right answer to most questions: either true or false; either right or wrong. Standardized mass testing, which is more convenient for teachers and institutions to score and tabulate, unfortunately pushes us further away from our individual creativity. We need to remember that not everything can be scored simply as true or false. Life is full of essay questions.

I used to deliver newspapers when I was 12 years old. I'd get up at 3:30 a.m. to deliver the papers, then go back to sleep at about 5 a.m. I'd wake up again at about 7:30 a.m., and it felt like I'd slept all night long. I did this so I wasn't tired during the day, but more importantly, being able to go back to bed served as a reward for getting up and doing my job well. I trained my mind to use this as incentive and it motivated me to get up every day. It was as if I didn't even have a paper route!

A more normal, conventional way of thinking would have led me to get up just in time to do my route, and then get ready for school as soon as I was done. That's the way everyone else did it, so it must have been the right way to do it. Right?

Not necessarily! Just because something has been done a certain way for a long time doesn't mean it's the only way, or even the best way, to do it. It just means that's the way most people do it. And remember, if we want to be our best, we must strive to do things differently than most people, because most people don't utilize their talents or reach for their highest potential!

Unfortunately, our creative abilities have become crippled to a greater or lesser extent by being conditioned with the "right or wrong" view of the world. If we ever hope to recapture our natural creative abilities, we must work hard to exercise our minds and shake loose the creativity-deadening shackles of the past.

Let's not make the mistake of thinking of creativity as something that only artists, musicians, and poets need. We *all* need it. Creativity spawns ideas. Ideas, by definition, are abstract and intangible in nature. Yet every business in the world was originally built on the foundation of someone's single creative idea. Remember, IBM started out as a fish scale company. And every business depends on a steady, ongoing stream of ideas to solve problems and meet goals. Even if we're the hardest headed, most pragmatic business people in the world, we need creative ideas just to survive, let alone get ahead. Once we understand that, we'll begin to look at creativity differently.

Creativity is the life blood of businesses. Creativity is what feeds them and enables them to grow. It's their fuel. Without ongoing creativity and ideas, all companies would wither away. All great advances and inventions have come from individual creativity, from someone doing things differently than before, from someone with a good idea.

It takes creativity to make great things happen.

Norman Vincent Peale once said, "Imagination ... is the true magic carpet." Albert Einstein also placed a high value on creativity. He said, "Imagination is more powerful than knowledge."

These two powerful minds understood the value of the creative mind. Once we come to the same understanding, and work to revitalize our innate creativity, our minds can become powerful tools in achieving our dreams.

Remember:
- Look for the "second" right answer.
- Bring your creativity out of its coma.

Pink Vanilla

A unique example of how creativity can be used to change perceptions and solve problems is illustrated in a story about a young man who was in charge of his younger brother and sister for the weekend.

He was doing everything he could to make them happy: bowling, miniature golf, movies, anything that would entertain them and keep the peace! He promised them that he'd get their favorite flavor of ice cream – vanilla – at the nearby ice cream shop if they behaved.

They behaved, and as he went in to the shop, the children reminded him that they both wanted vanilla. Once inside, he found out that the shop was out of vanilla. Did he panic? No. He bought strawberry instead, came out smiling, handed his younger brother and sister the cones, and said, "Look – it's pink vanilla!"

This is an example of using our powers of creativity to alter our perceptions. This kind of thinking is very important as we unlock our potential and *Change!*

Let's work to regain and develop our creative talents. Let's look for pink vanilla.

Remember:
- See "pink vanilla."

Box Surprise

Creativity is often merely the ability to see things in a new perspective. For example, how many squares are in the diagram on this page? Actually, there are 30 squares.

This exercise shows us that sometimes all we need is someone to suggest that there *is* more than what is readily apparent. It's beneficial to be around people who can help us expand our vision, change our perspective, and see things in new ways.

Remember:
- Look further.

Make a Third

I once heard a little story that went something like this:

"Two friends and I were walking down the roadway of life one day and came upon a fork in the road. One friend took the road to the left, while the other took the road to the right.

"I chose to make a third."

I challenge us all to "make a third" road in our lives. Let's think about the things we're doing now that conform to the norm, and then give ourselves permission to be *us*, which means being unique.

We need to discover who we really are and then be that person. This will open up vast horizons of creativity in our lives.

Each of us is a one-of-a-kind, an original, a limited edition of one. We may be similar to some people in some ways, but no one is exactly like us, and no one – and I mean no one – can offer the world exactly what we can offer. We are not only creative, but what we can offer through that creativity is unlike anything anyone else on earth can offer. However, we have to find out who we really are and *be* who we are before we can access those unique gifts.

So let's "make a third" road in our lives – our own unique path to creativity and fulfillment.

Remember:
- "Make a third" in your life.

Kick-Starting Our Creativity

Creativity takes energy. It's difficult to be creative when our batteries are low. Conversely, when our energy level is high, we're more likely to come up with creative ideas and solutions.

We can keep our creative motors running in high gear by maintaining high energy levels. To set the stage for this kind of high-energy living, the basic rules of health should be followed: eat right and get plenty of exercise and sleep.

We should then learn how to compress our time; doing what we do with focus and intensity; doing more with the time we have. Every so often, we need to "whack yourself on the side of the head" or give ourselves "a kick in the seat of the pants," as Roger von Oech suggests. A lot of people are walking around "asleep." Let's wake ourselves up and get some enthusiasm!

We should start energizing ourselves the moment we wake up. Zig Ziglar has a great idea on how to start the day. As soon as we wake up, we sit right up on the edge of our beds, clap our hands, and say, "It's going to be a great day!" After that, we get off our beds immediately. We don't sit there and think about it. We don't reset our alarm clocks and lie back down. We get out of bed right then!

There's a great day out there waiting for us every morning. If we attack it with energy and creativity, we'll be surprised how far we'll go.

Remember:
- Kick-start your creativity into action.

Riddle My Mind

I love riddles. I love the kind that are played like a game of Twenty Questions, where we are only allowed to ask "yes or no" questions to attempt to solve the riddle.

The purpose of such riddles is to exercise the parts of our minds that typically lie dormant. They say we only use 10 percent of our brains. This exercise helps us utilize more.

Here's an example:

A man is dead, lying in the middle of a field. There are no tracks leading to him, or from him. How did he die?

We can ask specific questions in order to learn points of fact that we aren't aware of yet. Presently, we know a man is dead, he's lying in a field, and there are no tracks leading to or from him. But that's all we know for sure.

These exercises teach us the importance of looking at a given situation freshly and objectively, without preconceived notions. They are designed to teach us to move step by step closer to an answer or a solution – thinking and pondering instead of making assumptions and jumping to conclusions.

The sleuths in mystery and detective series on TV like *Columbo* and *Murder She Wrote* utilize this same sort of process, as did such characters as Sherlock Holmes and Hercule Poirot.

If you guessed that the man was a parachuter and his parachute didn't open, you were right. But think of the things that were taken for granted or assumed immediately, without asking. For instance, "Was he a 'normal' man? Did he have any handicaps? Did the type of field he was in matter? Does it matter how long he was dead?"

Here are some other riddles. Do your best to stretch your creativity and figure them out. (The answers are grouped together after the riddles.)

The Hanging Man

A man is dead, hanging by a rope around his neck. His body is three feet above the ground. The rope is attached to a hook in the middle of the ceiling of the room. The room is 20 feet by 20 feet. There is nothing else in the room. No one other than the dead man came in or out of the room. How did he die? (He didn't jump.)

Sam and Sally

Sally is lying on the floor dead. Glass and water are all around her. Sam is looking over Sally. Who is Sam, who is Sally, and how did Sally die?

15th Floor

A man lives on the 15th floor of an apartment building. He wakes up every morning, goes into the elevator, and presses "1st floor." He gets off the elevator on the 1st floor and goes to work. When he gets home at night, he walks into the building, goes into the elevator and presses "7th floor." He then gets out on the 7th floor and takes the stairs the rest of the way up to the 15th floor. Why?

Two Men in a Bar

Two men are in a bar, drinking. They order the same drink from the same bartender. They are given exactly the same drink. One guzzles his down and walks out. The other sips his slowly, and while sitting there after approximately 30 minutes, drops over dead. Why did one man walk out unharmed while the other dropped over dead if they drank exactly the same drink?

Gun Drink

A man walks into a bar and asks the bartender for a drink. Instead of pouring a drink, the bartender pulls out a gun and points it at the man's head. The man says, "Thank you," and walks out satisfied. Why?

Paper Puzzler

A man is dead, sitting in the driver's seat of his car that was parked in a grocery store parking lot. He was shot in the head. The bullet came through his side window. There are about two inches of snow on the ground and you can see tracks leading to and from the car. There is a piece of paper lying behind the car. What is the piece of paper, what kind of tracks are they, who killed him, and why?

Answers and Explanations to the Riddles:

The Hanging Man

The man brought a three-foot high block of ice with him when he went into the room. He used it to stand up and reach the hook. The ice melted, he died, and the water evaporated.

Sam and Sally

Sam is a cat and Sally is a fish. Sam swatted at Sally in her glass fishbowl and knocked the bowl and Sally to the ground. Sally died on the floor surrounded by glass and water from her fishbowl. (The key here is to avoid assuming the obvious: that Sam and Sally were humans. Asking specific questions about Sam and Sally is the ideal way to figure this one out.)

15th Floor

The man is a midget and can't reach the 15th floor button on the elevator. He can only reach as high as the 7th floor button. Therefore, he gets off at the 7th floor and walks the rest of the way up to his floor, which is the 15th.

Two Men in a Bar

Both men got drinks that had ice laced with poison in the middle. The man that drank his down quickly survived because the ice didn't have time to melt and release the poison. The man who died sipped his drink slowly, giving the ice time to melt and release the poison into his drink. The bartender wanted to kill both men, but succeeded in killing only one.

Gun Drink

The man had hiccups, which the bartender helped him get rid of by putting the gun to his head and frightening him out of them.

Paper Puzzler

The piece of paper has a car's license number written on it. The tracks to and from the dead man's car were wheelchair tracks. The driver of the car was involved in a hit-and-run accident, in which he paralyzed a man and killed his wife. The killer was the man he paralyzed – a man who was now in a motorized wheelchair. He had kept the license number, and had later found the same car and driver parked in a parking lot. He drove his wheelchair over to the car and shot him through the window.

Remember:

•   Riddles exercise the mind and help us tap into the other dormant nine-tenths of our brains.

Key 11:

FEEDING OUR SOULS

Wealth and Worth

I learned many lessons during my rise to the top. I learned even more during my fall. One of the most important things I learned was the difference between *wealth* and *worth*.

A lot of people put a great deal of stock in money. The fact is, it's a lousy measuring stick.

It's easy to compare ourselves to others using criteria that matter the least – like money, the size of our homes, the number of cars we drive, and so on.

But there's something I hope we always remember: *Wealth has nothing to do with worth.* Our personal worth is measured by who we are, not what we have accumulated. Some of the wealthiest people I know are also the most superficial. Some of the "richest" people I know have very little money or material possessions.

But they have great *worth*.

Personal worth comes from strong roots based on values, morals, ethics, and a sincere love for our fellow man here on earth.

During my troubles, I began to understand that integrity, strength of character, and humility were the qualities I should be striving for, instead of focusing solely on becoming wealthy. These qualities became major goals of mine.

The Bible tells us that "the meek shall inherit the earth." It hit me that if I pursued spiritual strength and values, and worked to adopt and practice those characteristics, then wealth would take care of itself.

Wealth will be more likely to gravitate to us, and will come to us with less stress, as money becomes a by-product of living to our fullest spiritual, moral, and ethical potentials.

What I'm suggesting is nothing more than what has been

taught by the great spiritual leaders throughout history: we must seek to become people of *worth*, and the wealth we need will follow.

It's a question of priorities. Let's keep them straight!

Remember:
• Worth is more valuable than wealth.

The Spiritual Perspective

Spirituality is a very broad and often very personal topic to discuss. But I want to discuss it in this book, because frankly, it's too important not to.

Literally defined, spirituality is a sensitivity toward religious values. When we acquire a sense of spirituality, our perspectives on *everything* in life changes. It changes our thinking, and our vision, making them vaster and deeper than before. It changes the way we see our own lives, the world around us, and our personal and business relationships. It helps us think long-term, rather than basing our lives and actions on short-term thinking.

A sense of spirituality provides balance and helps us stay "centered" on a daily basis. It also helps us to be humble. Acknowledging a higher power – a supreme existence – will humble us in the sense that we will be aware of our dependence on a Supreme Being as well as the foolishness of many things we previously felt were so vitally important. At the same time, we will begin to get in touch with the infinite power and potential within ourselves. This type of humility – the ability to see how small yet big, how weak yet strong we really are – is a characteristic that will be vital in our rise to success.

In the ups and downs of my own life, spirituality has taught me to never look at things with finality – to never think that "it's all over," or that "this is the end." Possessing spirituality and believing in a Supreme Being (a higher power, one bigger and stronger than myself) has made me see things from an eternal perspective.

If we can succeed at obtaining this type of perspective through our spirituality, I'm here to say that we'll never look at today, next week, next year, or even old age and death as the end of our existence. We'll begin to live life differently – with more responsibility and accountability.

The perspectives of our spirits literally affects everything we undertake in our lives, and how we respond to events and situations. It also serves to put the magnitude of our current challenges in perspective, reducing the worry and stress associated with them. Possessing spiritual roots gives us something to hold onto when times get tough and it appears as if nothing else is there for us.

I have often asked myself where I would be without my faith. Most likely, I would be lost, broke, destitute ... maybe even dead. Whenever I started to feel like I wasn't going to make it, whenever I started to feel sorry for myself, I just thought about Job, or someone else who experienced difficult challenges.

My spiritual base helped me because I *knew* that the low point I was experiencing was not "the end." I knew that it, too, would eventually pass. No, it didn't happen quickly, but my strong eternal beliefs allowed me to survive until things did change.

Remember:
- Work to build personal spirituality.

"Perfect" Is a Verb – Not a Noun

Many of us are looking for "the perfect" job, or "the perfect" spouse, or "the perfect" house. But perfection is not a destination – it's a process. It's not a noun, but a verb.

I believe that one of our main purposes in life is to work toward our individual perfection and to do the things that will help us progress toward our full, individual potential. I believe that we take this responsibility upon ourselves when we come to this earth, and that we'll be happy to the extent that we make this happen. In my own life, I feel the responsibility to work to improve myself every day.

If we all take a good, close look at ourselves, openly and candidly, I think we'll all realize that we have a lot to work on – more than enough to keep us busy throughout this lifetime!

This process of perfecting ourselves is long and arduous. Often, it's discouraging when we realize how far we still have to go. But we shouldn't think of it like that. We should think of it as the ongoing journey that it is, rather than a destination alone. We should take joy in this journey, delighting in every step we take forward along our paths, and feeling good about every inch of progress we make. Then, and only then, will seeking perfection be an exciting process that will give us a lifetime of satisfaction.

Remember:
* Appreciate the process of perfecting yourself.

Going to Church

A friend once shared the following illustration with me in order to make a point.

Imagine that you work for a rich man who really likes you. One day this man announces that he is giving his immensely valuable company to you. He is not *selling* it to you. He is *giving* it to you. And all he asks in return is that you go to his house every Sunday and have dinner with him.

In the beginning, you go there faithfully and without fail every Sunday for dinner. You're excited about taking over his company and you're truly grateful for all he has done for you.

But as time goes on, you become more involved in other activities and the Sunday get-togethers start to get in your way. In fact, you begin to see them as a chore. You soon start skipping an occasional Sunday dinner with him. Then, slowly, over time, you stop going altogether.

This story illustrates how many people feel about church attendance. They think it gets in the way of more important or more pressing activities. They struggle to go, then give up and stop going, except for perhaps at Christmas and Easter, which they consider to be "important" times of the year.

Going to church can give us an uplifting feeling. The feeling can be the same even when we attend churches of different denominations with friends, or when we travel. After all, I believe everyone is worshiping the same Supreme Being.

It can be argued that we can worship Him from our homes. But that unique and special fellowship, friendship, and sharing can't always be found within the confines of our homes in the same way it can at church. We may be able to find more peace and tranquility at home, but not the mutual bonding with our fellow brothers and sisters. Also, churches are much like schools

– they are places where we can go to become spiritually educated.

If you're not doing it already, I challenge you to begin this very week to attend the church of your choice on a regular basis. (If you're skeptical, remember this universal rule: "If it can possibly do some good, and can't do any harm, then do it.") I can assure you that you'll reap many wonderful benefits that will exert a positive influence in your life.

Remember:
•   If you feel you should go to church, go!

The Power of Prayer

We should get into the habit of praying or meditating.

It's important to find a quiet time to do this. I suggest praying the first thing in the morning and the last thing in the evening.

As soon as we wake up in the morning, we can roll out of bed and onto our knees before doing *anything* else. This is a time, before we get involved in the cares and hectic pace of the day, when we will be most receptive to inspiration and guidance. We can do the same at night (in reverse order, of course), making prayer the last thing we do before going to bed.

Our morning prayers will start our days out right, helping us focus and gather the inner peace and power we'll need to be successful at the things that lie before us. Our evening prayers will help us see things in their proper perspective, evaluate our actions and thoughts of the day, and know what we need to do to improve ourselves. They will also help us calm our minds in preparation for a good night's sleep.

We don't need to worry about how to pray or what to say – just do it! People pray (and meditate) in many different ways, but the main point is to open our hearts and minds to the Supreme Being. Once this happens, we can express our gratitude for the blessings we've received, and ask for solutions to problems or for needed blessings for ourselves and those around us.

Life is tough enough. Why go it alone? I know I can't make it on my own. I don't know anyone who can. The essence of spirituality is that there is a higher being that loves us, cares about us, and is always with us. But unless we stay in touch through regular prayer, we'll forget about this and begin to feel very much alone in life.

By praying and asking for help on a regular basis, I am reminded that I am not alone. I *know* I can make it. I hope everyone will pray for that same conviction. It will make a world of difference!

Remember:

*   Wake up ten minutes early every morning and start the day with prayer and quiet time.

Service With a Smile

I believe one of the reasons we're here in this world is to help others. Giving genuine service is wonderful. Have you ever helped someone and felt that you benefitted more by giving the service than they did by receiving it? I have. I think that's the way it works.

We all need to give ourselves to others by giving service. I'm not saying we should run out and volunteer all our time at a hospital or nursing home (although those are good ways to do it). Service can take on many forms and can be given virtually anywhere. It can be stopping on the freeway to pick up a muffler that fell off a car and is now a hazard on the road. It can be helping a friend move without having to be asked. It can be visiting an elderly, home-bound person just to chat, coaching a Little League team, asking a neighbor to go along when we go boating, and so on.

There are many opportunities for service around us every day. If we look around, we'll always know when we're being "of service" by the warm, irreplaceable feeling we get inside. It's a satisfying, gratifying, rewarding feeling.

Let's get in touch with this sensation and become more service-oriented. Let's make it a way of life so that when the opportunity presents itself we'll be tuned in and ready to serve when our help is needed. Cervantes said, "He that gives quickly, gives twice."

Making service a way of life will help us reach our goals quicker. People will sense our warmth, sincerity, and strength of character when they meet us. They'll feel comfortable around us – like they've known us for years. This is a real asset in the business world, and will yield immeasurable benefits in our careers.

Most transactions or business of any type occurs when one party is comfortable with the other party. This feeling of comfort comes from within. It is manifested in business dealings. Many people have said they don't really know why they decided to do business with a certain individual or company, except they were comfortable with them. I believe that service, when it's given out of a genuine desire to help the other person, helps to create this feeling in others.

Remember:
- Find ways to give service.
- Enjoy the rewards of giving.

The Rarest Qualities

These days, the more "traditional" qualities of honesty, sincerity, integrity, and strength are becoming quite rare and very valuable.

If we have these qualities, we'll rise higher than we can imagine. Genuineness cannot be fabricated. A person's face tells all. We can often zero in on the type of person someone is simply by looking at that person's face – especially the eyes.

Someone who is kind, caring, and helpful; someone who helps others; someone who lives a balanced, healthy life; someone who lives in accordance with spiritual guidelines; someone who gives time and money to good causes and does other worthy things ... you can see these things on a person's face. It's impossible to hide the treasures they've found: peace, serenity, balance, and completeness. You can feel it.

True and everlasting happiness is found within – not outside in the world of materialism and instant gratification. Let's work to make ourselves people of uncommon quality and substance. Let's cultivate in our hearts and minds these rare qualities. By doing so, we can become our own best attribute for success.

Remember:
- Genuineness shines through in our countenances.
- Look in the mirror. How do you come across?

THE DOOR TO *CHANGE!* IS UNLOCKED

A Time for Action

Spencer W. Kimball had a little sign on his desk that said, "Do it!" That sign was his philosophy – a philosophy that kept him energetic and made him extremely effective as the leader of a worldwide organization well into his 80s.

Now that you've read *Change!*, I challenge you to "Do it!" Go over the notes I hope you've made as you've read this book. Pick out something you've learned or some suggestion that you know will improve your life – and start working on it today. Choose something else tomorrow, or next week, then something else the following day or week, and so on.

The point is, if you don't *do it*, it won't get done. All your reading will be wasted, and you won't accelerate your journey to your goals one iota.

One wise man stated, "When all is said and done, more is said than done." Don't let this be the case in your life.

Get out and get started. Take the plunge. Make the leap of faith. Even if it's a tiny step toward self-improvement, take it. Now!

Your life will never be the same.

Before I close this book, I'd like to offer you a few final thoughts on the following closing pages to help you on your way. But first ...

Remember:
*   Now is the time to "Do it!"

A Creed
For Those Who Have Suffered

I asked God for strength, that I might achieve.
I was made weak, that I might learn humbly to obey.
I asked for health, that I might do greater things.
I was given infirmity, that I might do better things.
I asked for riches, that I might be happy.
I was given poverty, that I might be wise.
I asked for power, that I might have the praise of men.
I was given weakness, that I might feel the need of God.
I asked for all things, that I might enjoy life.
I was given life, that I might enjoy all things.
I got nothing I asked for, but everything I had hoped for.
Almost despite myself, my unspoken prayers were answered.
I am, among men, most richly blessed!

– Anonymous

Some of My Favorite Quotes

"A minute's success pays the failure of years." – Robert Browning

"A goal is a dream with a date on it." – Unknown

"The reasonable man adapts himself to the world; the unreasonable one persists in trying to adapt the world to himself. Therefore, all progress depends on the unreasonable man." – George Bernard Shaw

"New opinions are always suspected and usually opposed – without any other reason but because they are already not common." – John Locke

"Far better it is to dare mighty things though checkered by failure, than to live in the grey twilight that knows neither victory nor defeat." – Theodore Roosevelt

"Success is to be measured not so much by the position that one has reached in life as by the obstacles which he has overcome while trying to succeed." – Booker T. Washington.

"What lies behind us and what lies ahead of us are nothing compared to what lies within us." – Anonymous

"The significant problems we face cannot be solved at the same level of thinking we were at when we created them." – Albert Einstein

An Invitation

Now that you've read *Change!* and have made the commitment to "Do it!" you're going to see some wonderful changes in your life.

You're going to become a real-life success story!

Because success stories about real people have helped me overcome adversity and find success, I've decided to help others achieve the same results by compiling a book of stories about people who have successfully implemented the ideas and principles in this book.

When you're ready, I'd like to include your story. Please write and tell me how the keys in this book have helped you unlock the door to success and *Change!* – even if it is just in one small area of your life – and we may interview you for our upcoming *Change! II* book and video.

Until I hear from you, I wish you the very best that life has to offer. I would wish you the best of luck, but that's not necessary. If you do your part, you won't have to depend on luck to unlock the doors to your most treasured goals. *You* can make it happen. You can *Change!* Work to be your Personal Best. And most of all, remember:

Always believe in yourself! Change is power!

– John Ross
Inside Corporation
4255 East Charleston Boulevard, Suite 188
Las Vegas, Nevada 89104-6640
800-379-3420

Thank You in Advance!

To learn more about the Inside Corporation's maximal perspective *Change!* program for inmates, please call, write, or fax us.

If you would like to make a donation to cover the cost of distributing these books to inmates, please send us $10. If you would like to help us even further, please do so by sponsoring an adult or juvenile facility and covering the cost of their books. We teach and distribute books to between 50 and 250 inmates per facility.

Please contact us at:

The Inside Corporation
4255 East Charleston Boulevard, Suite 188
Las Vegas, Nevada 89104-6640
800-379-3420